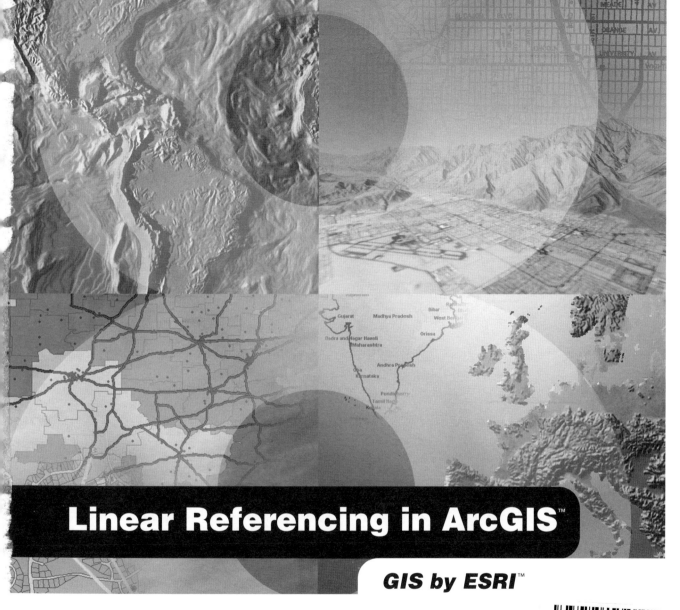

Linear Referencing in ArcGIS™

GIS by ESRI™

DATA CREDITS

Highways and streets map—Maryland Department of Transportation State Highway Administration, Baltimore, Maryland

Transit map—Parsons Brinckerhoff Quade & Douglas, Inc., Los Angeles, California

Railways map—Parsons Brinckerhoff Quade & Douglas, Inc., Los Angeles, California

Oil and gas exploration map—TGS-NOPEC Geophysical Company, Houston, Texas

Pipelines map—M.J. Harden Associates, Inc., Kansas City, Missouri

Water resources map—Center for Research in Water Resources, University of Texas at Austin

Hatching map 1—New York State Department of Transportation, Albany, New York

Hatching map 2—TGS-NOPEC Geophysical Company, Houston, Texas

WRITER

Patrick Brennan

Contents

1 Introduction   1

Who uses linear referencing?   2

Tips on learning about linear referencing   8

2 Quick-start tutorial   9

Exercise 1: Organizing your data in ArcCatalog   10

Exercise 2: Creating and calibrating route data   11

Exercise 3: Displaying and querying routes   19

Exercise 4: Displaying and querying route events   26

Exercise 5: Editing routes   32

3 Linear referencing   39

The need for linear referencing   40

Routes and measures   43

Route locations and route events   44

Linear referencing and topology   45

4 Creating route data   47

Route data   48

Creating route feature classes   54

Creating routes from existing lines   61

Calibrating routes with points   67

Migrating route data to a geodatabase   73

5 Displaying and querying routes and events   77

The route identifier field   78
Querying route data   79
Hatching   83
Displaying hatches   91
Manipulating the text on hatches   99
Hatch styles   101
Route measure anomalies   104
Dynamic segmentation   105
Adding route events   107

6 Editing routes   109

Adding the Route Editing toolbar   110
Creating routes from existing lines   111
Calibrating routes with points   117
Route measures   119
Remeasuring routes   121

7 Creating and editing event data   125

Creating and editing event data   126
Creating event tables in ArcCatalog   132
Overlaying events   136
Aggregating events   139
Transforming event measures   141
Locating points along routes   144
Locating polygons along routes   146
Editing event tables in ArcMap   148

Glossary   153

Index   161

Introduction

IN THIS CHAPTER

- Who uses linear referencing?

- Tips on learning about linear referencing

Many organizations collect data about linear *features*, such as highways, city streets, railroads, rivers, and pipelines as well as water and sewer networks. In most geographic information systems (GIS), these features are modeled in two dimensions, using x,y coordinates. While these systems work well for maintaining features with static characteristics, these organizations have realized that their linear features often have characteristics that are more dynamic in nature. To handle this, these organizations have developed one-dimensional linear referencing systems to model their data.

How these organizations store and utilize their linear referencing data varies not only between the organizations themselves but also between the departments within the organizations. Because of this variance, there is a need for flexible tools to create, display, query, analyze, and distribute linear referencing data.

ESRI® ArcGIS™ software contains a series of easy-to-use tools, wizards, and dialog boxes that assist you in meeting your linear referencing needs. In this book, you will learn how to create, calibrate, edit, display, and query the data used in linear referencing.

Who uses linear referencing?

Most applications that use linear features can benefit from linear referencing. The following pages outline a few examples.

Highways and streets

Agencies that manage highways and streets use linear referencing in a variety of ways in their day-to-day operations. For example, linear referencing is useful for assessing pavement conditions; maintaining, managing, and valuing assets (traffic signs and signals, guard rails, toll booths, loop detectors, etc.); organizing bridge management information; and reviewing and coordinating construction projects. Linear referencing also helps facilitate the creation of a common database that traffic planners, traffic engineers, and public works analysts can use for cross-disciplinary decision support.

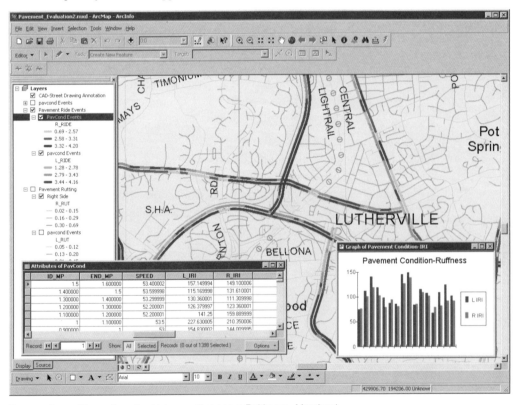

Pavement conditions along the highways that serve Baltimore, Maryland

Transit

Linear referencing is a key component in transit applications and facilitates such things as route planning and analysis; automatic vehicle location and tracking; bus stop and facility inventory; rail system facility management; track, power, communications, and signal maintenance; accident reporting and analysis; demographic analysis and route restructuring; ridership analysis and reporting; and transportation planning and modeling.

Corridor study showing the number of traffic accidents along an 18-mile stretch of the I-710 Freeway in Los Angeles County

Railways

Railways use linear referencing to manage key information for rail operations, maintenance, asset management, and decision support systems. Linear referencing makes it possible, for example, to select a line and track and identify milepost locations for bridges and other obstructions that would prevent various types of freight movement along the route. Further, dynamic segmentation can be used to display track characteristics as well as to view digital images of bridges and obstructions.

Analyzing rail clearances along the Hudson rail line in downstate New York

Oil and gas exploration

The petroleum industry manages tremendous volumes of data used in geophysical exploration. Seismic surveys, or shotpoint data, are used to help understand the underlying geology in an area. The nature of seismic data is that it must be represented as both a linear object—the seismic line—and a collection of point objects—the shotpoint. Both the seismic line and the individual shotpoints have *attributes*, both must be maintained at the same time, and both are used in modeling applications. Linear referencing helps solve this problem.

Posting and labeling seismic lines and shotpoints in the Gulf of Mexico off of the Louisiana coast

Pipelines

In the pipeline industry, linear referencing is often referred to as stationing. *Stationing* allows any point along a pipeline to be uniquely identified. As such, stationing is useful for collecting and storing information regarding pipeline facilities, both inline and physical inspection histories, regulatory compliance information, risk assessment studies, work history events, and geographic information, such as environmentally sensitive areas, political boundaries (state, county, etc.), right-of-way boundaries, and various types of crossings.

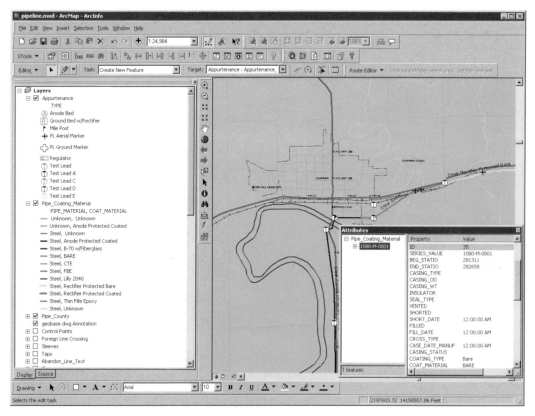

Pipeline coating material types in rural Kansas

Water resources

In hydrology applications, linear referencing is often called river addressing. *River addressing* allows objects, such as field monitoring stations, which collect information about water quality analysis, toxic release inventories, drinking water supplies, flow, and so on, to be located along a river or stream system. Further, the measurement scheme used in river addressing allows for the measurement of flow distance between any two points on a flow path.

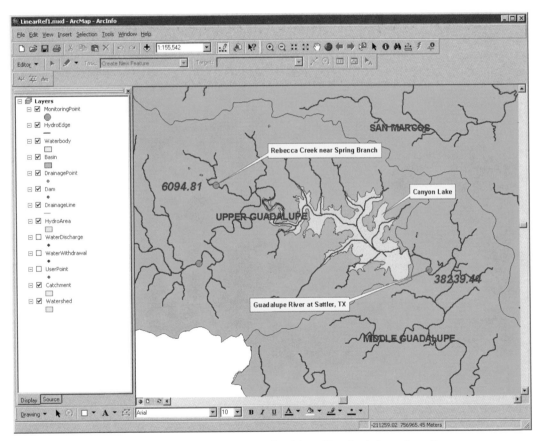

Monitoring stations along the hydrology network of the Guadalupe River basin in southern Texas

Tips on learning about linear referencing

If you're new to GIS, take some time to familiarize yourself with ArcGIS. The books *Using ArcCatalog*, *Using ArcMap*, *Editing in ArcMap*, and *Building a Geodatabase* contain tutorials to show you how to create, edit, manage, and display GIS data.

Begin learning about linear referencing and dynamic segmentation in Chapter 2, 'Quick-start tutorial', in this book. In Chapter 2, you will learn how to create and calibrate route data, display and query route and event data, and edit route data. ArcGIS comes with the data used in this tutorial, so you can follow along step by step at your computer. You can also read the tutorial without using your computer.

Finding answers to your questions

Like most people, your goal is to complete your tasks while investing a minimum amount of time and effort in learning how to use software. You want intuitive, easy-to-use software that gives you immediate results without having to read pages of documentation. When you do have a question, however, you want the answer quickly so you can complete your task. That's what this book is all about—getting you the answers you need when you need them.

This book describes how to accomplish linear referencing tasks. Although you can read this book from start to finish, you'll likely use it more as a reference. When you want to know how to do a particular task, such as identifying a route location, just look it up in the table of contents or index. What you'll find is a concise, step-by-step description of how to complete the task. Some chapters also include detailed information that you can read if you want to learn more about the concepts behind the tasks. You may also refer to the glossary in this book if you come across any unfamiliar GIS terms or need to refresh your memory.

Getting help on your computer

In addition to this book, the ArcGIS Desktop Help system is a valuable resource for learning the software. To learn how to use Help, see *Using ArcMap*.

Contacting ESRI

If you need to contact ESRI for technical support, see the product registration and support card you received with ArcGIS or refer to 'Contacting Technical Support' in the 'Getting more help' section of the ArcGIS Desktop Help system. You can also visit ESRI on the Web at *www.esri.com* and *support.esri.com* for more information on linear referencing and ArcGIS.

ESRI education solutions

ESRI provides educational opportunities related to geographic information science, GIS applications, and technology. You can choose among instructor-led courses, Web-based courses, and self-study workbooks to find educational solutions that fit your learning style. For more information, go to *www.esri.com/education*.

Quick-start tutorial

2

IN THIS CHAPTER

- **Exercise 1: Organizing your data in ArcCatalog**

- **Exercise 2: Creating and calibrating route data**

- **Exercise 3: Displaying and querying routes**

- **Exercise 4: Displaying and querying route events**

- **Exercise 5: Editing routes**

ArcGIS has the tools you need for linear referencing applications. The easiest way to start learning about linear referencing is to complete the exercises in this tutorial. Before you start, however, it is assumed you know the fundamentals of ArcToolbox™, ArcCatalog™, and ArcMap™ software. For more information, see *Using ArcToolbox*, *Using ArcCatalog*, *Using ArcMap*, and *Editing in ArcMap*.

For this tutorial, imagine that you work in the GIS department of a highway authority responsible for the maintenance and safety of your region's highways. In the exercises to follow, you will perform some of the linear referencing tasks typical to such a person. Specifically, you will use ArcToolbox to create and recalibrate route data. Next, you will learn how to display and query your newly created route data in ArcMap. After that, you will discover how easy it is to display and query your route event data in ArcMap. Lastly, you will learn how to edit your route data in ArcMap.

To complete many of the exercises in this tutorial, you will need to have an ArcInfo™ license. Feel free, however, to read through the exercises to familiarize yourself with the linear referencing functionality in ArcGIS.

Work on this tutorial at your own pace. The exercises build on one another, so it is assumed that you will complete them in order. This tutorial includes five exercises, each of which takes five to 30 minutes to complete.

The study area for this tutorial is Pitt County, North Carolina. The data was compiled from various sources and has been modified to suit the needs of the exercises. The reliability and suitability of the information, therefore, cannot be guaranteed.

Exercise 1: Organizing your data in ArcCatalog

The exercises in this chapter use the tutorial data distributed with ArcGIS. The default install location of the data is C:\arcgis\ArcTutor\LinearReferencing. Some of the following exercises require that you change the data. You will, therefore, need to have write access to the data. If you do not want to change the data at the default location or you do not have write access, you will need to copy the LinearReferencing folder to a new location before you start the exercises.

Connecting to the data

In ArcCatalog, folder connections let you access directories on local disks or shared folders on the network. Further, database connections allow you to access the contents of a database.

1. Start ArcCatalog by either double-clicking a shortcut installed on your desktop or using the Programs list in your Start menu.

2. Click the Connect To Folder button on the Standard toolbar.

3. Navigate to the LinearReferencing folder on the local drive where you installed the tutorial data.

4. Click OK.

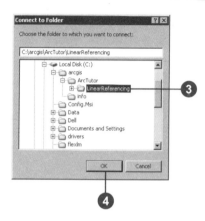

The new folder connection is now listed in the Catalog tree. You will now be able to access all of the data needed for the remaining exercises in this tutorial via the new connection.

Exercise 2: Creating and calibrating route data

The first thing you will need for any linear referencing project is accurate route data. In this exercise, you will first create a route feature class by merging input line features that share a common route identifier. This is done with the Create Routes Wizard, which is in ArcToolbox.

Next, you will recalibrate the newly created route feature class using a point feature class that stores route and measure information as attributes. This is done with the Calibrate Routes Wizard, which is also in ArcToolbox.

Creating route data

The Create Routes Wizard is used to specify the input line feature class, the route identifier field, the method used to set the route measures, and the output feature class. Note that the input feature classes can be any supported format. This includes coverage, shapefile, personal and enterprise geodatabase, and *computer-aided design (CAD)* data.

1. Start ArcToolbox by either double-clicking a shortcut installed on your desktop or using the Programs list in your Start menu.

2. Double-click the Create Routes Wizard in ArcToolbox in the Linear Referencing toolset of Data Management Tools.

There are several ways to set the input feature class. You can drag a line feature class from the ArcCatalog tree and drop it onto the text box, click the Browse button to open the ArcCatalog minibrowser and navigate to the feature class, or simply type the full pathname to the feature class in the text box.

The tutorial instructions will simply ask you to type names and paths into the appropriate text boxes. Feel free, however, to use any of the available techniques.

3. Type "C:\arcgis\ArcTutor\LinearReferencing\ PITT.mdb\PITT\base_roads" for the Input Feature Class.

4. Click the Route Identifier Field dropdown arrow and click ROUTE1. The values in the route identifier field uniquely identify each route.

5. Click Next.

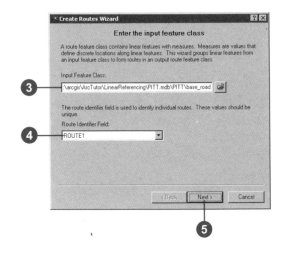

This panel asks you to specify how the route measures will be obtained. There are three choices:

- The geometric lengths of the input features are used to accumulate the measures.

- A value stored in a measure field is used to accumulate the measures.

- The values stored in from- and to-measure fields are used to set the measures.

You will use the third method.

6. Click Use two fields from the input feature class.

7. Click the From-Measure field dropdown arrow and click BEGMP1.

8. Click the To-Measure field dropdown arrow and click ENDMP1.

9. Click Next.

The output routes can be written to a shapefile or a geodatabase feature class. You will be writing to a new feature class in the same feature dataset as the input feature class.

10. Click Feature class in a geodatabase.

11. Click Next.

If your input features have a defined projection, the Create Routes Wizard will preserve this projection. You can choose to change the projection information for the output, in which case the features will automatically be projected. Note that you cannot change the projection if you are writing to an existing feature dataset.

Whenever writing routes to a geodatabase, you should always set the m domain. A default m domain will be calculated for you, but this might not accurately reflect your needs.

12. Type "C:\arcgis\ArcTutor\LinearReferencing\ PITT.mdb" for the Output Geodatabase.

13. Click the dataset dropdown arrow and click the PITT dataset.

14. Type "routes" for the name of the new feature class.

15. Click Change Settings.

16. Click Change.

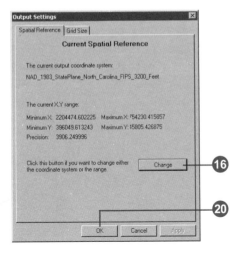

17. Click the M Domain tab.

18. Type "-1000" for the Min and "10000" for the Precision. These settings will ensure that your route measures will be accurate to four decimal places.

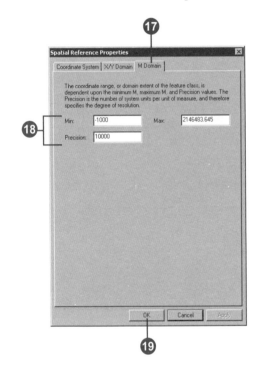

19. Click OK.

20. Click OK on the Output Settings dialog box.

At this point, you will have returned to the Enter the output feature class panel.

21. Click Next on the Create Routes Wizard.

Not all features from the input feature class have route and measure information. These features represent roads that are not currently maintained by the highway authority and do not need to be included in the output route feature class. You will exclude these features from the route creation process by specifying a query.

22. Click Use only those features that satisfy a query.

23. Click the Click to define a query button.

24. Type "[ROUTE1] < > 0" in the text box.

25. Click OK.

26. Click Next on the Create Routes Wizard.

27. Review your settings and click Finish.

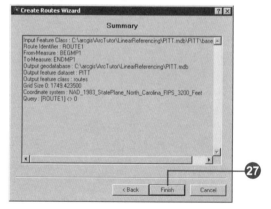

Calibrating route data

Imagine that at some point in the future, the highway authority's road maintenance crew acquired a distance measuring instrument (DMI) so that they could accurately record mileage information along the highways. For a sample set of highways, the crew went out and captured mileage information approximately every 1/10 of a mile. The results of this effort were stored as points in a shapefile, where the route and mileage information was stored as attributes.

In the next section of this tutorial, you will use the Calibrate Routes Wizard to adjust the measures of the routes you just created to match those of the points in the shapefile. The result will be written to a new feature class.

The Calibrate Routes Wizard is used to specify the input route feature class, the route identifier field, the input point feature class, the measure field, the methods used to set the route measures, and the output feature class. Note that the input route feature classes can be any supported format. This includes coverage, shapefile, personal and enterprise geodatabase, and CAD data.

Note that in addition to being able to adjust the measures of existing routes, the Calibrate Routes Wizard can also be used to create new routes by merging unmeasured input line features using a common route identifier and setting the measure information using the point attributes. To mimic the acquisition of more accurate data over time, however, the process was split into two separate tasks for this exercise.

1. Double-click the Calibrate Routes Wizard in ArcToolbox in the Linear Referencing toolset of Data Management Tools.

2. Type "C:\arcgis\ArcTutor\LinearReferencing\ PITT.mdb\PITT\routes" for the Input Feature Class.

3. The values in the route identifier field uniquely identify each route. Click the Route Identifier Field dropdown arrow and click ROUTE1.

4. Click Next.

5. Type "C:\arcgis\ArcTutor\LinearReferencing\ Calibration_Points.shp" for the Point Feature Class.

6. Click the Point Identifier Field dropdown arrow and click ROUTE1.

7. Click the Measure dropdown arrow and click MEASURE.

A tolerance can be specified to limit how far a calibration point can be from its route. Points outside the tolerance will not be used by the calibration process. The tolerance is expressed in the same units as the route feature class's coordinate system.

8. Type "5" for the tolerance. This is more than enough for the data that is being used here.

9. Click Next.

If your point features have a projection that differs from the route features, the Calibrate Routes Wizard will project the points to match the routes before the calibration process starts.

Either whole or partial routes can be calibrated. You can choose to interpolate between the input points, extrapolate before the input points, extrapolate after the input points, or use any combination of these three methods.

Note that the Extrapolate before calibration points, Interpolate between calibration points, and Extrapolate after calibration points check boxes are checked by default.

10. Click Next.

The output routes can be written to a shapefile or a geodatabase feature class. You will be writing a new feature class in the same feature dataset as the input routes.

11. Click Feature class in a geodatabase.

12. Click Next.

13. Type "C:\arcgis\ArcTutor\LinearReferencing\ PITT.mdb" for the Output Geodatabase.

14. Click the dataset dropdown arrow and click the PITT dataset.

15. Type "routes_new" for the name of the new feature class.

16. Click Change Settings.

17. Click Change.

Note that whenever you create a feature class in a geodatabase, you should always check to make sure that the spatial domains are correct. In this tutorial, you will only check the m domain.

18. Click the M Domain tab.

19. Type "-1000" for the Min and "10000" for the Precision. These settings will ensure that your route measures will be accurate to four decimal places.

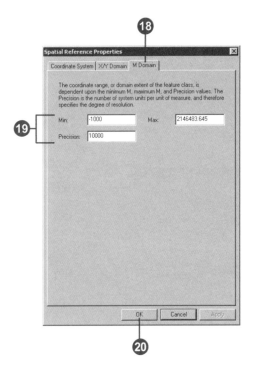

20. Click OK.

21. Click OK.

At this point, you will have returned to the Enter the output feature class panel.

22. Click Next.

23. Click Next.

24. Review your settings and click Finish.

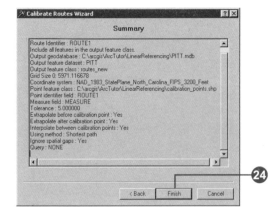

In this exercise, you learned how to create a route feature class by merging input line features that shared a common identifier and how to adjust the route measures using measure information stored in a point shapefile. For more information on creating and calibrating route data, see Chapter 4, 'Creating route data'.

Exercise 3: Displaying and querying routes

In this exercise, you will add the route data you created in Exercise 2 to an existing map document and symbolize it. You will then

- Set the route identifier field.

- Add the Identify Route Locations tool to a toolbar.

- Identify route locations.

- Find route locations.

- Display route measure anomalies.

Opening an existing map document

Before you can complete this exercise, you must start ArcMap.

1. Double-click a shortcut installed on your desktop or use the Programs list in your Start menu to start ArcMap.

2. Click Open from the ArcMap File menu.

3. Click the Look in dropdown arrow in the Open dialog box and navigate to the folder where you installed the data for this tutorial.

4. Double-click Ex3.mxd. ArcMap opens the map.

This map contains the following layers in a data frame called Pitt County:

calibration_points	The points used in Exercise 2 to recalibrate the route measures
base_roads	All of the roads in Pitt County
city boundaries	The boundaries of the cities in Pitt County
county boundary	Pitt County boundary

The map currently displays the city boundaries and county boundary layers. Their check boxes are checked in the table of contents. The calibration_points layer is checked, but scale suppression has been set. It will only be visible when you zoom in to a scale beyond 1:25,000.

5. Click the check box for the base_roads layer in the table of contents.

You will now see all of the roads in Pitt County. This includes roads not maintained by the highway authority. The roads maintained by the highway authority were written to the routes feature class.

Adding route data to your map

1. Click the Add Data button on the ArcMap Standard toolbar.

2. Click the Look in dropdown arrow and navigate to where you installed tutorial data. Double-click Pitt.mdb and double-click the Pitt feature dataset.

3. With the Ctrl key pressed down, select both the routes and routes_new feature classes.

4. Click Add. You will see two new layers in the table of contents.

Changing the display symbol

The colors and symbols ArcMap chose to display for the routes layer might make it difficult to see where the route features are located. It is easy to change the colors and symbols used to display features in ArcMap.

1. Click the line symbol in the table of contents for the routes layer to display the Symbol Selector dialog box.

2. Scroll down until you find a symbol you like and click it.

3. Click OK. Your routes layer will be displayed with the symbol you chose.

4. Repeat steps 1 through 3 for the routes_new layer.

You can also open the Symbol Selector dialog box by right-clicking the layer in the table of contents, clicking Properties, and clicking the Symbology tab. To simply change the color of a symbol, right-click the symbol in the table of contents to display the color palette. For more information on changing display symbols, see *Using ArcMap*.

Setting the Route Identifier field

ArcMap knows whenever route data has been added to a map and exposes some additional layer properties. One of these properties is the Route Identifier field. This field uniquely identifies each route.

Setting the Route Identifier field is not required. Doing so, however, reduces the number of steps required to use many of the ArcMap Linear Referencing dialog boxes, wizards, and tools.

1. Right-click the routes layer in the table of contents and click Properties.

2. Click the Routes tab.

3. Click the Route Identifier dropdown arrow and click ROUTE1.

4. Click OK.

5. Repeat steps 1 through 4 for the routes_new layer.

Adding the Identify Route Locations tool

ArcMap gives you the ability to point to a route in a map and find the route identifier and measure value at that location. In this part of the exercise, you will use the Identify Route Locations tool to inspect the measures on the routes you created in Exercise 2.

The Identify Route Locations tool does not appear on any toolbar by default. You will have to add it to one.

1. Click Customize from the ArcMap Tools menu.

2. Click the Commands tab.

3. Click Linear Referencing in the Categories list.

4. Drag the Identify Route Locations tool to the toolbar of your choice (e.g., the Tools toolbar).

5. Click Close.

Identifying route locations

In ArcMap, a bookmark is a saved map location. A bookmark containing some of the calibration points used in Exercise 2 to recalibrate the routes has been created for you.

1. Point to Bookmarks from the ArcMap View menu and click Calibration Points.

When ArcMap moves to the saved location, the calibration points appear with labels that represent the measure values for each point. The reason they appear when the bookmark has been used is because scale suppression was set on the layer. For more information on scale suppression, see *Using ArcMap*.

2. Click the Identify Route Locations button.

3. Move the mouse pointer over one of the calibration points and click. Route locations from both the routes and routes_new layers will be identified.

4. Click the route node for each of the route layers.

The numeric value listed for each of these nodes corresponds to the value stored in the Route Identifier field, which you set in a previous section of this exercise. Note that the measure value for the two routes differs. Note further that the measure value for the routes_new layer corresponds closely to the measure value of the calibration point you clicked (the closer you are to a calibration point, the closer the measure will be).

5. Right-click the route node for one of the layers and explore the context choices available to you.

6. Uncheck the check box for the calibration_points layer in the table of contents to make it not visible. It will not be used any further in this exercise.

7. Close the Identify Route Location Results window.

Finding route locations

In many linear referencing applications, you will discover that you will often need to find a location along a route. For example, you may need to find where an accident occurred along a highway. On a paper map, it is hard to find a route location. This is because route measures are typically not shown. In ArcMap, finding a route location is made easy.

1. Click the Find button on the ArcMap Tools toolbar.

2. Click the Route Locations tab.

3. Click the Route Reference dropdown arrow and click routes_new.

Notice that the field listed in the Route Identifier dropdown arrow corresponds to the Route Identifier field you set previously in this exercise.

4. Type "30000121" in the Route text box.

5. Type "5" in the Location text box.

6. Click Find.

7. Right-click the route location that was found and explore the context choices available to you.

8. Close the Find dialog box.

Displaying route measure anomalies

In most linear referencing applications, route measure values are expected to follow a set of rules. For example, you might expect that route measures always increase over the course of a route. ArcMap has the ability to show you where route measures do not adhere to the behavior you expect. These are known as *route measure anomalies*.

1. Click the Full Extent button on the ArcMap Tools toolbar.

2. Right-click the routes layer in the table of contents and click Properties.

3. Click the Routes tab.

4. Check Show where measures do not increase.

5. Click the Line Symbol button and select a line symbol you like. Do the same for the marker symbol.

6. Click OK.

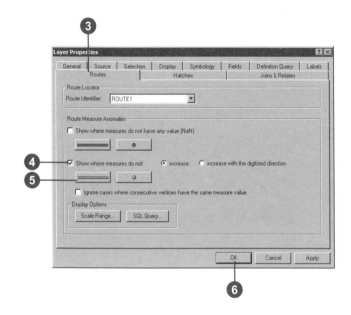

Remember that the routes feature class was created from the base_roads feature class in Exercise 2. There are a few digitizing errors and a few attribute errors that caused the measure anomalies to exist in the routes feature class. Route measure anomalies can be fixed with ArcMap route editing tools. For more information on route editing tools, see Chapter 6, 'Editing routes'.

Exercise 4: Displaying and querying route events

In this exercise, you will create a new event table that represents where injury accidents occurred along sections of poor-quality pavement. To do this, you will first use the Add Route Events dialog box to display the accident location and pavement quality event data on your map. You will then use the Select By Attributes dialog box to select the injury accidents and poor-quality pavement locations. Finally, you will use the Route Events GeoProcessing Wizard to create a new event table whose records represent where injury accidents occurred along poor-quality pavement.

Opening an existing map document

Before you can complete this exercise, you must start ArcMap.

1. Double-click a shortcut installed on your desktop or use the Programs list in your Start menu to start ArcMap.

2. Click Open from the ArcMap File menu.

3. Click the Look in dropdown arrow in the Open dialog box and navigate to the folder where you installed the data for this tutorial.

4. Double-click Ex4.mxd. ArcMap opens the map.

This map contains the following layers in a data frame called Pitt County:

routes_hwy	Shapefile copy of routes_new feature class you created in Exercise 2
county boundary	Pitt County boundary
accident	Point event table storing accident information
pavement	Line event table storing pavement information
base_roads	All of the roads in Pitt County

Displaying point events on your map

The accident table is a point event table. Point events occur at a precise point location along a route. In this section of the exercise, you will display the accident event data as a layer.

1. Click Add Route Events from the ArcMap Tools menu.

2. Click the Route Reference dropdown arrow and click routes_hwy.

3. Click the Route Identifier dropdown arrow and click ROUTE1.

4. Click the Event Table dropdown arrow and click accident.

5. Click the Route Identifier dropdown arrow and click ROUTE1.

6. Click the Measure dropdown arrow and click MEASURE.

7. Click OK.

A new layer—accident Events—has been added to your map.

Displaying line events on your map

The pavement table is a line event table. Line events differ from point events in that they have two measure fields that define a portion of a route. The procedure for adding line events to your map is almost the same as adding point events.

1. Click Add Route Events from the ArcMap Tools menu.

2. Click the Route Reference dropdown arrow and click routes_hwy.

3. Click the Route Identifier dropdown arrow and click ROUTE1.

4. Click the Event Table dropdown arrow and click pavement.

5. Click the Route Identifier dropdown arrow and click ROUTE1.

6. Click Line Events.

7. Click the From-Measure dropdown arrow and click BEGIN_MP.

8. Click the To-Measure dropdown arrow and click END_MP.

9. Click OK.

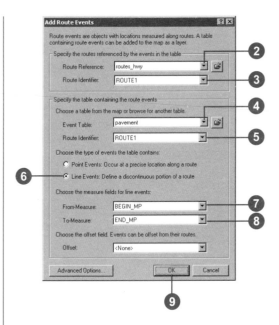

A new layer—pavement Events—has been added to your map.

Querying events

Layers based on an event table can be queried in many ways. They can be identified by clicking them, they can be selected by dragging a box or clicking them on the map, they can be selected by clicking them in an attribute table, and they can be selected using a Structured Query Language (SQL) expression. You will use the Select By Attributes dialog box to input SQL expressions to select the event records needed for this exercise. Specifically, you will select injury accidents and poor quality pavement.

1. Click Select By Attributes from the ArcMap Selection menu.

2. Click the Layer dropdown arrow and click accident Events.

3. Type the following in the text box:
   "NUM_INJURY" > 0

4. Click Apply.

5. Click the Layer dropdown arrow and click pavement Events.

6. Type the following in the text box: "RATING" < 50

7. Click Apply.

8. Click Close.

There are many events selected on your map. In the next section of this exercise, you will use the Route Events GeoProcessing Wizard to intersect the two event layers. The result will be a table that contains the injury accidents that happened on poor-quality pavement. All attributes from both inputs are maintained.

Intersecting event layers

1. Click Route Events GeoProcessing Wizard from the ArcMap Tools menu.

2. Intersect two route event layers is the default. Click Next.

3. Click the input route event layer dropdown arrow and click accident Events.

4. Click the overlay route event layer dropdown arrow and click pavement Events.

5. Click Next.

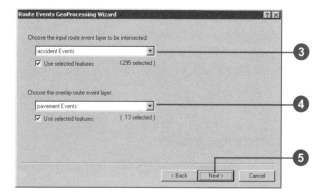

6. Type "C:\arcgis\ArcTutor\LinearReferencing\AccPav.dbf" for the output route event table.

7. Click Finish.

A new layer—AccPav Events—will be added to your map. It will be hard to see, however, because the accident and pavement event layers are still visible.

8. Turn off the accident and pavement layers by clicking their check boxes in the table of contents.

You will now see only the injury events that occurred along poor quality pavement. Each of these new events has all of the attributes from both the accident and pavement tables.

For more information on the display and query of events or the spatial analysis of events, see Chapter 5, 'Displaying and querying routes and events', and Chapter 7, 'Creating and editing event data'.

Exercise 5: Editing routes

There are a number of tools in ArcMap that make the interactive creation and editing of route measures easy. In this exercise, you will create a new route from a selected set of linear features and set its identifier. You will then convert the measures of this newly created route from feet to miles. Lastly, you will recalibrate the route using known measure values at specific locations on your map.

Opening an existing map document

Before you can complete this exercise, you must start ArcMap.

1. Double-click a shortcut installed on your desktop or use the Programs list in your Start menu to start ArcMap.

2. Click Open from the ArcMap File menu.

3. Click the Look in dropdown arrow in the Open dialog box and navigate to the folder where you installed the data for this tutorial.

4. Double-click Ex5.mxd. ArcMap opens the map.

Adding route data to your map

You will use one of the route feature classes you created in Exercise 2 to complete this exercise.

1. Click the Add Data button on the ArcMap Standard toolbar.

2. Click the Look in dropdown arrow, navigate to where you installed tutorial data, double-click Pitt.mdb, and double-click the Pitt feature dataset.

3. Double-click the routes_new feature class. You will see a new layer in the table of contents.

Adding the toolbars, editing, and setting the target feature class

The toolbars necessary to complete this exercise might not be visible.

1. Click the Editor Toolbar button on the ArcMap Standard toolbar to add the Editor toolbar to ArcMap.

2. Click the Editor menu, point to More Editing Tools, and click Route Editing.

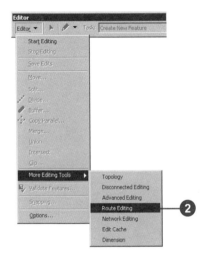

3. Click the Editor menu and click Start Editing.

4. Click the Target dropdown arrow and click routes_new.

Making a route from selected features

The highway authority has been informed that it will now be responsible for maintaining a road that it previously had not been maintaining. It is necessary, therefore, to select the appropriate features from the base_roads feature class and make a route in the routes_new feature class out of them.

The Make Route command creates a new route in the target feature class by merging a selected set of line features and setting the measure values. The selected line features do not need to be from the target feature class.

1. Click Select By Attributes from the ArcMap Selection menu.

2. Click the Layer dropdown arrow and click base_roads.

3. Type the following in the text box:
   [FENAME] = 'Cornerstone Row'

4. Click Apply.

5. Click Close.

Nine features from the base_roads feature class are now selected.

6. Right-click the base_roads layer in the table of contents, point to Selection, and click Zoom To Selected Features.

7. Click the Make Route button on the Route Editing toolbar.

8. Click the Start Point button.

9. Click the mouse pointer on the map near the upper-right corner of the selected set of features. This is where the output route's measures will begin.

10. Click Make Route.

The new route will flash when it is being created. During the route creation process, the selected lines will be unselected, and the new route will be selected. This is so you can set the new route's attributes.

Setting the Route Identifier

Because the newly created route is selected, you can now set the route identifier. The route identifier uniquely identifies each route.

1. Click the Attributes button on the Editor toolbar.

2. Click the ROUTE1 value and type "40001777".

3. Press Enter.

4. Close the Attributes dialog box.

Converting route measure units

When you created the new route, you accepted the default method for setting the route measures. This method accumulates the geometric length of the input line features and uses the length as the measure. Because the coordinate system of the feature class is State Plane Feet, this means that the measures on the new route are feet. However, the measures on all other routes in the feature class are miles.

1. The newly created route should still be selected. If it is not, select it.

2. Click the Task dropdown arrow and click Modify Feature.

The selected feature will now be loaded into the edit sketch.

3. Click the Sketch Properties button. Note the measure values.

4. Close the Edit Sketch Properties dialog box.

5. Right-click anywhere over the edit sketch, point to Route Measure Editing, and click Apply Factor.

6. Type "0.00018939" in the Factor text box and press Enter. This converts feet to miles.

At this point, you have only made changes to the edit sketch, not the route feature.

7. Press F2 to finish the edit sketch. Alternately, right-click anywhere over the edit sketch and click Finish Sketch.

Your route measures are now in miles. You can verify this by double-clicking the selected route to bring it into the edit sketch, right-clicking anywhere over the sketch, and clicking Properties. Note that this is an alternate way to perform Steps 2 and 3.

Recalibrating a route

So far in this exercise, you have created a route and transformed its measures from feet to miles. Imagine that at some point the maintenance crew went out into the field and recorded the actual mileage for this new route. The mileage was captured every time the new route intersected with another route from the same feature class. In this section of the exercise, you will recalibrate the newly created route based on this mileage information.

1. The newly created route should still be selected. If it is not, select it.

2. Click the Editor menu and click Snapping.

3. Check the End check box next to the routes_new layer.

4. Close the Snapping Environment dialog box. It will not be used again in this exercise.

With the snapping environment set, you will be able to create calibration points that are snapped to the end vertex of the features in the routes_new layer, thereby ensuring accuracy of the route measures at the calibration points. Setting the snap environment, however, is not necessary for the Calibrate Route command to work.

5. Click the Task dropdown arrow and click Calibrate Route Feature.

6. Click the Calibrate Route button on the Route Editing toolbar.

The Calibrate Route dialog box is now on the screen, but it is empty. Your next task is to digitize the calibration points.

7. With the Calibrate Route dialog box open, click the Sketch tool on the Editor toolbar.

8. Click along the route at nine different places to create the calibration points. The locations of the calibration points are indicated in the graphic below.

9. Type the New M value (see values in graphic below) for each calibration point.

10. Click Calibrate Route.

Saving your edits

Once you have completed the steps in this exercise, you can choose to save or discard your edits by stopping the edit session.

1. Click the Editor menu and click Stop Editing.

2. Click Yes to save your edits or No to discard your edits.

In this exercise, you first learned how to create a route from a selected set of line features. Next, you converted the route measures from feet to miles. Lastly, you learned how to recalibrate a route using calibration points you digitized on the map.

For more details about the route editing tools outlined here or for information on tools not discussed in this chapter, see Chapter 6, 'Editing routes'.

Linear referencing

3

IN THIS CHAPTER

- **The need for linear referencing**

- **Routes and measures**

- **Route locations and route events**

- **Linear referencing and topology**

Highways, city streets, railroads, rivers, pipelines, and water and sewer networks are all examples of linear features. *Linear features* typically have only one set of attributes. *Linear referencing*, however, provides you with an intuitive way to associate multiple sets of attributes to portions of linear features. With linear referencing, your ability to understand, maintain, and analyze linear features is greatly improved.

This chapter outlines the way linear features are modeled in ArcGIS. It then introduces you to what linear referencing is, explains why it is needed, and outlines the concepts necessary to develop linear referencing applications. Once you understand the concepts introduced in this chapter, you can refer to later chapters in this book to use the wide range of linear referencing functionality in ArcGIS.

The need for linear referencing

Geographic data is modeled in a number of ways: as a collection of features in *vector* format, as a grid of cells with spectral or attribute data in raster format, or as a set of triangulated points modeling a surface in triangulated irregular network (TIN) format.

Data that has a discrete location with a defined shape and boundary is modeled using the vector format. In this format, data is represented by features. Features are stored in feature classes. Every feature has a geometry associated with it. This geometry is stored in a special field that is typically called shape. A feature can have one of these types of geometries: point, multipoint, polyline, or polygon. Each geometry is composed of two-dimensional (x,y) or three-dimensional (x,y,z) geographic coordinates.

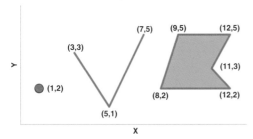

In the vector format, geographic data is stored as a feature that has a geometry type of point, multipoint, polyline, or polygon.

The vector format works well for modeling features with static characteristics, such as parcel boundaries, water bodies, and soil characteristics. Some applications, however, require the ability to model the relative location along various linear features, such as highways, city streets, railroads, rivers, pipelines, and water and sewer networks.

Because of this need, one-dimensional measuring systems, such as river mile and route milepost, have been devised. These systems simplify the recording of data by using a relative position along an already existing linear feature. That is, location is given in terms of a known linear feature and a position, or *measure*, along it. For example, route I-10, mile 23.2, uniquely identifies a position in geographic space without having to express it in x,y terms.

When data is linearly referenced, multiple sets of attributes can be associated with any portion of an existing linear feature, independent of its beginning and end. These attributes can be displayed, queried, edited, and analyzed without affecting the underlying linear feature's geometry.

The need to visually represent features on a map whose coordinates are not geographic but are recorded as a relative distance along another linear feature led to the development of dynamic segmentation. *Dynamic segmentation* is the process of displaying linearly referenced features on a map. For more information on dynamic segmentation, see Chapter 5, 'Displaying and querying routes and events'.

Storing features as relative locations

Locating a spatial feature along another linear feature would typically be done using a planar (two-dimensional) referencing system of x,y coordinates.

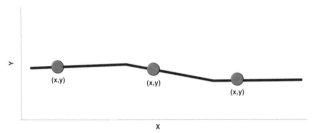

Locating accidents using x,y coordinates

This works well in some applications. In others, however, locations along linear features are referred to in terms of their distance from a known point. For example, it makes much more sense to record the location of an accident as occurring at "12 miles from the beginning of the interstate" rather than at "1659060.25, 1525238.97".

To determine a location along a linear feature, a system of measurement is required. When a measurement system is stored with a linear feature, any location along that linear feature can be expressed in terms of the measure values.

Locating accidents using measure values

In addition to making data more intuitive, storing data as a relative location along a linear feature has the added benefit of ensuring that spatial phenomena you know to be along a linear feature is mapped as such. For example, in the absence of an accurate basemap, locating accidents using x,y coordinates may end up displaying accidents that do not fall along the road network. This cannot happen if the accidents are stored as measurements along the linear features of the road network.

Segmented data

The *vector model* of data storage dictates that you must split a linear feature wherever its attribute values change. Certain linear features, however, have attributes that change frequently. The pavement condition of a road, for example, changes as pavement deteriorates and is subsequently repaired. To accurately reflect the changes in pavement condition, you will have to split some features and merge others.

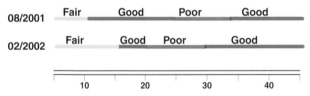

To attach attributes describing pavement quality, it is necessary to split a linear feature at several locations to reflect changes in data. Over time, pavement quality changes, requiring features to be split or merged.

Segmenting the linear features becomes more problematic when you need to store other attributes, such as traffic volumes, lane information, surface material, speed limits, and accident locations. Every time these attributes change, the road will need to be further subdivided. With all the required segmenting, it is evident that the linear features will be so subdivided that the data will be difficult, if not impossible, to maintain.

Storing multiple sets of attributes for one feature is made possible using linear referencing.

ArcGIS uses route event tables to store linearly referenced attributes. Event rows are composed of a route identifier, measure values indicating a location, and one or more attributes describing the location. For more information on route event tables, see 'Route locations and route events' in this chapter.

Because events simply reference measure locations along linear features, they are edited and maintained independently of the linear features. For more information on maintaining event data, see Chapter 7, 'Creating and editing event data'.

Routes and measures

When linearly referenced features in ArcGIS are referred to, the terms routes and route events are used. A *route* is any linear feature, such as a city street, highway, river, or pipe, that has a unique identifier and a measurement system. This measurement system defines discrete locations along the linear feature. For more information on route events, see 'Route locations and route events' in this chapter.

A route is a linear feature with a unique identifier and a measurement system.

A collection of routes with a common system of measurement can be stored in a single *feature class*—for example, a set of all highway routes in a county. In a geodatabase, many feature classes containing routes can be stored in a single *feature dataset*. For example, a state's department of transportation (DOT) might maintain a feature dataset with feature classes for milepost routes, reference marker routes, and so on.

A feature dataset can have multiple feature classes that store routes.

Linear features and, therefore, routes are stored in a feature class whose geometry type is a polyline. A *polyline* is an ordered collection of paths that can be connected or disjointed. Polylines are used to represent such things as roads, rivers, and contours.

Polyline with one path   Polyline with multiple, connected paths   Polyline with multiple, disjointed paths

A polyline is an ordered collection of paths that can be connected or disjointed.

Polylines can have a measurement system stored with their geometry. Instead of being a collection of segments with x,y coordinates, a measured polyline's segments have x,y and m (measure) or x,y,z and m values. When a measure value is unknown, it is listed as NaN (not a number).

Polylines can have a measurement system stored with their geometry. Measures can be unknown (NaN).

It is important to note that although many applications use measures to represent increasing distances along a linear feature, measure values can arbitrarily increase, remain constant, or decrease.

Measure values are independent of the *coordinate system* of a feature class. That is, the measure values are not required to be in the same units as the feature class's x,y coordinates. For example, features stored in a feature class whose coordinate system is *Universal Transverse Mercator (UTM)* meters might have measure values stored in feet or miles.

Route locations and route events

A *route location* describes a discrete location along a route (point) or a portion of a route (line). A point route location uses only a single measure value to describe a discrete location along a route. An example of a point route location is "mile 3.2 on the I-91." A line route location uses both a from- and a to-measure value to describe a portion of a route. "Mile 2 to mile 4 on the I-91" is an example of a linear route location.

When route locations—and their associated attributes—are stored in a table, they are known as *route events* or simply *events*. Events are organized into tables based on a common theme. For example, five event tables containing information on speed limits, year of resurfacing, present condition, signs, and accidents can reference highway routes.

Route event tables

Because there are two types of route locations, there are two types of route event tables: point and line.

A *route event table*, at a minimum, consists of two fields: a route identifier and a measure location. The route identifier field is a numeric or character value used to identify the route to which an event belongs. A measure location is either one or two fields that describe the positions along the route at which the event occurs. These values can be defined as any numeric item.

An event table can be any type of table that ArcGIS supports. This includes INFO™, dBASE®, geodatabase tables, delimited text files, and database management system tables accessed via an OLE DB connection.

Point events

Point events occur at a precise point location along a route. Accident locations along highways, signals along rail lines, bus stops along bus routes, and pumping stations along pipe lines are all examples of point events. Point events use a single measure value to describe their location.

GAUGES

REACH	MP	GAUGE_ID
A123	12	A1
A123	30	A2
A123	47	A3
B456	9	B1
B456	35	B2

Measure location

Route identifier

Events are located along a route using their route location information. Here, point events representing flow gauges along river reaches are shown.

Line events

Line events describe portions of routes. Pavement quality, salmon spawning grounds, bus fares, pipe widths, and traffic volumes are all examples of line events. Line events use two measure values to describe their location.

HABITAT

REACH	FMP	TMP	SPECIES
A123	5	13	SALMON
A123	15	25	STEELHEAD
A123	30	52	SALMON
B456	17	25	STEELHEAD

Measure location

Route identifier

Events are located along a route using their route location information. Here, line events representing fish habitats along river reaches are shown.

Linear referencing and topology

Within an organization, there may be many departments that use route event data. Each department will collect event data using the route measurement system that best suits its needs. Within a state DOT, for example, the safety department might collect accident location events using a reference marker system of measurement, while the maintenance department might collect pavement quality information using a mile post system of measurement. Each system is known as a *linear referencing method*.

A route in ArcGIS can only store one system of measurement. In many organizations, therefore, there is a need to maintain multiple route feature classes—one for each linear referencing method.

A topology facilitates the use of multiple linear referencing methods.

The ability to manage these feature classes in an integrated fashion is critical.

In GIS technology, *topology* is the model used to describe how features share geometry. It is also the mechanism for establishing and maintaining topological relationships between features and feature classes. ArcGIS implements topology through a set of validation rules that define how features share geographic space and a set of editing tools that work with features that share geometry in an integrated fashion.

By defining a topology, organizations can achieve the data integration between route feature classes they require. For more information on topology, see *Building a Geodatabase* and *Editing in ArcMap*.

Creating route data

4

IN THIS CHAPTER

- **Route data**

- **Creating route feature classes**

- **Creating routes from existing lines**

- **Calibrating routes with points**

- **Migrating route data to a geodatabase**

Before embarking on any linear referencing project, you will need route data. This data may not exist, may exist but without the appropriate measure system defined, or may exist in a format you do not wish to use.

ArcGIS supports routes in three formats: coverage, shapefile, and geodatabase. ArcCatalog and ArcToolbox provide you with the tools necessary to create, calibrate, and migrate route data from one supported format to another.

In this chapter, you will learn how to:

- Create new route feature classes.

- Create route feature classes from existing lines.

- Calibrate routes using points.

- Migrate routes from one format to another.

Route data

A *route* is a linear feature that has a unique identifier and measurement system stored with it. Routes can be stored in coverages, shapefiles, and personal and ArcSDE® geodatabases.

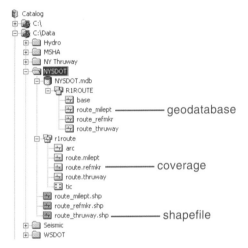

Routes can be stored in coverages, shapefiles, and geodatabase feature classes.

ArcCatalog and ArcToolbox contain tools for creating route data in shapefiles and geodatabases. In addition to the ability to create empty route feature classes for later digitizing or importing, there are tools for creating routes by merging existing line features, calibrating route data with points, and migrating route data from one format to another. When a route feature class is stored in a geodatabase, there are special storage considerations.

There are tools for creating coverage route data, but they will not be discussed in this chapter. ArcInfo Workstation remains the best place to create coverage route data. For more information on creating coverage route data, see the ArcInfo Workstation online Help.

Merging linear features to create routes

It is possible to create routes by merging linear features that share a common identifier. There are two scenarios for how the route measures will be set:

- Measure values for the input features are not known.
- Measure values for the input features are known.

Measure values are not known

When route measure values are not known, they can be generated either by accumulating the digitized length or by accumulating a numeric attribute value of the input features. If you choose to use digitized length, the units of the output route measures will be the same as the output coordinate system (feet, meters, etc.). If you choose to use a numeric attribute, the output route measures can be any units you want.

When routes are created in this manner, you control the direction measures are assigned to the routes by specifying the coordinate priority of the starting measure. The coordinate priority can be upper left, upper right, lower left, or lower right. These options are determined by placing the minimum bounding rectangle around the input features that are going to be merged to create one route.

Measure values are obtained by accumulating the values in the MILES field. Note that the digitized direction of the input features does not matter because a starting priority is given. In this example, the starting priority is lower left.

Routes with multiple, disjointed parts are supported. A route representing a road, for example, might have the same name on either side of a river. For situations like this, you can choose to ignore spatial gaps between parts when creating routes. If you choose to ignore spatial gaps, route measures will be continuous when a disjointed route is created. If you want the spatial gap incorporated in the measures, the gap distance is the straight-line distance between the endpoints of the parts. The units of the gap will be that of the output coordinate system, which may or may not be the same as the measure units.

OID	Shape	RKEY	FR_M	TO_M
0	Polyline	1	0	1.1
1	Polyline	1	1.1	2.3
2	Polyline	1	2.3	3.2

OID	Shape	RKEY
0	PolylineM	1

Measure values are obtained by using the values in the FR_M and TO_M fields. Note that the digitized direction of the input features determines the direction of the output route.

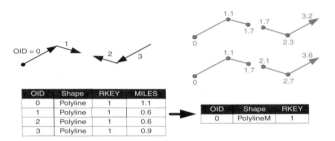

OID	Shape	RKEY	MILES
0	Polyline	1	1.1
1	Polyline	1	0.6
2	Polyline	1	0.6
3	Polyline	1	0.9

OID	Shape	RKEY
0	PolylineM	1

When creating disjointed routes, you can choose to have the measures be continuous or discontinuous. In this example, the starting priority is lower left.

Measure values are known

When measure data already exists as attributes of the input linear features, it is possible to create routes that inherit this measure information. For example, two fields may exist that store from- and to-mile information.

When using this method, it is important to orient each input linear feature in the direction of increasing measure to prevent routes that have measures that do not always increase.

Calculating route measures using points

When route measures are inaccurate, events will not be located properly. A route representing a highway, for example, might be 10.5 miles long. A bend in the highway might have its measure value set to 6.1 miles. In reality, however, the bend in the highway occurs at mile 6.5. Events on this route, especially near the bend, will be located incorrectly.

It is possible to adjust route measures to correspond with known measure locations using a procedure called calibration. *Calibration* adjusts route measures by reading measure information stored as an attribute in a point feature class. Each point falls on the particular route it calibrates or within a given tolerance. Many points may be used to calibrate a single route.

During the calibration process, a new vertex is created where the calibration points intersect the route. The measure value on these new vertices corresponds to the measure value stored as a point attribute. The measure values on other preexisting route vertices can be interpolated and/or extrapolated.

The calibration process creates a new vertex for every point within the specified tolerance. The measure at each new vertex will correspond to the point's measure value. You control whether the remaining vertices will have their measure interpolated or extrapolated (see below).

Both whole and partial routes can be calibrated. You can choose to interpolate between the input points, extrapolate before the input points, extrapolate after the input points, or use any combination of these three methods.

In order for the measure value on a vertex to be interpolated or extrapolated, a calibration ratio is needed. There are two ways this ratio can be determined. The first method uses the shortest path distance between the input points.

Measure value at v1 is extrapolated as follows:
- distance (d1) between p1 and p2 is 14.31
- measure distance between p1 and p2 is 15-5 = 10
- calibration ratio is 14.31/10 = 1.431
- distance (d2) between p1 and v1 is 4.47

4.47/1.431 = 3.12
5-3.12 = 1.88

The measure value at v2 is interpolated as follows:
- distance (d1) between p1 and p2 is 14.31
- measure distance between p1 and p2 is 15-5 = 10
- calibration ratio is 14.31/10 = 1.431
- distance (d3) between p1 and v2 is 6.71

6.71/1.431 = 4.69
5+4.69 = 9.69

The measure value at v3 is interpolated as follows:
- distance (d4) between p2 and p3 is 11.628
- measure distance between p2 and p3 is 30-15 = 15
- calibration ratio is 11.628/15 = 0.775
- distance (d5) between p2 and v3 is 3.58

3.58/0.775 = 4.62
15+4.62 = 19.62

The measure value at v4 is interpolated as follows:
- distance (d6) between p3 and p4 is 7.16
- measure distance between p3 and p4 is 34-30 = 4
- calibration ratio is 7.16/4 = 1.79
- distance (d7) between p3 and v4 is 3.13

3.13/1.79 = 1.75
30+1.75 = 31.75

The measure value at v5 is extrapolated as follows:
- distance (d6) between p3 and p4 is 7.16
- measure distance between p3 and p4 is 34-30 = 4
- calibration ratio is 7.16/4 = 1.79
- distance (d8) between p4 and v5 is 7.16

7.16/1.79 = 4
34+4 = 38

The calibration ratio can be determined using the shortest path distance between the input points.

The second method uses the existing measure distance between the input points. This second method is useful when the length to measure ratio on the input route is not consistent and you are using the calibration process to fine-tune a route's measures.

When calibrating disjointed routes, you may choose to ignore the distance of the spatial gap between the parts. If you choose to ignore spatial gaps, route measures will be continuous. If you want the spatial gap incorporated in the measures, the gap distance is the straight-line distance between the endpoints of the parts. The units of the gap will be that of the output coordinate system, which may or may not be the same as the measure units. Ignoring spatial gaps is only a valid choice when using the shortest path distance method of calibration.

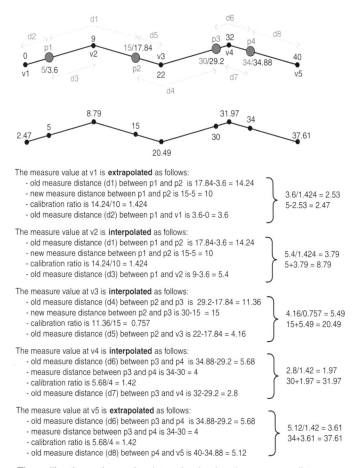

The measure value at v1 is **extrapolated** as follows:
- old measure distance (d1) between p1 and p2 is 17.84-3.6 = 14.24
- new measure distance between p1 and p2 is 15-5 = 10
- calibration ratio is 14.24/10 = 1.424
- old measure distance (d2) between p1 and v1 is 3.6-0 = 3.6

3.6/1.424 = 2.53
5-2.53 = 2.47

The measure value at v2 is **interpolated** as follows:
- old measure distance (d1) between p1 and p2 is 17.84-3.6 = 14.24
- new measure distance between p1 and p2 is 15-5 = 10
- calibration ratio is 14.24/10 = 1.424
- old measure distance (d3) between p1 and v2 is 9-3.6 = 5.4

5.4/1.424 = 3.79
5+3.79 = 8.79

The measure value at v3 is **interpolated** as follows:
- old measure distance (d4) between p2 and p3 is 29.2-17.84 = 11.36
- new measure distance between p2 and p3 is 30-15 = 15
- calibration ratio is 11.36/15 = 0.757
- old measure distance (d5) between p2 and v3 is 22-17.84 = 4.16

4.16/0.757 = 5.49
15+5.49 = 20.49

The measure value at v4 is **interpolated** as follows:
- old measure distance (d6) between p3 and p4 is 34.88-29.2 = 5.68
- measure distance between p3 and p4 is 34-30 = 4
- calibration ratio is 5.68/4 = 1.42
- old measure distance (d7) between p3 and v4 is 32-29.2 = 2.8

2.8/1.42 = 1.97
30+1.97 = 31.97

The measure value at v5 is **extrapolated** as follows:
- old measure distance (d6) between p3 and p4 is 34.88-29.2 = 5.68
- measure distance between p3 and p4 is 34-30 = 4
- calibration ratio is 5.68/4 = 1.42
- old measure distance (d8) between p4 and v5 is 40-34.88 = 5.12

5.12/1.42 = 3.61
34+3.61 = 37.61

The calibration ratio can be determined using the measure distance between the input points.

Special considerations for geodatabases

When you create a new standalone feature class or a feature class in a new feature dataset, you must specify a spatial reference. The spatial reference for a feature class contains its coordinate system—for example, geographic, UTM, and State Plane—and the spatial domains—x, y, z, and m. For more information on spatial references, see *Building a Geodatabase*.

You need to choose appropriate x, y, m, and perhaps z domains when creating route feature classes because they describe the maximum extent to which data can grow. For example, if you create a feature class with a minimum m value of 0 and a precision of 1,000, none of the routes in the feature class will be able to have measures that are less than 0. Further, all route measures will be accurate to three decimal places (a precision of 1,000 implies accuracy to three decimal places). Similar considerations apply to the x, y, and z domains.

All feature classes in a feature dataset share a common spatial reference. This means that the domains are shared as well. The exception to the rule is the m domain. Feature classes within the same feature dataset can have a different m domain. This is to account for the fact that different route feature classes might have different units of measure (for example, feet, meters, and miles). Whenever you create a route feature class in an existing feature dataset, you should always set an appropriate m domain.

Choosing an appropriate m domain

However route data is created, one important goal is to preserve measure accuracy. When data is stored in a geodatabase, all numeric values are converted to integers. Because of this, converting data to and from integer space can sacrifice measure accuracy if inappropriate m domain values are used.

To determine an appropriate m domain, you need to know both the route storage units and the route measure units. The route storage units reflect how accurately the route data was collected. For example, route measure data may be accurate to the foot, meter, or even decimeter level.

The route measure units refer to the units in which route locations are reported. For example, they may be feet, meters, miles, and so on. Route measure units have nothing to do with how accurately the route's data was collected and stored.

Precision is the multiplier that scales measure units into storage units. The lowest precision value you should use is the route measure units divided by the storage units. For example, if the route measure units are kilometers and there is meter-level accuracy, the lowest precision value you should use is 1,000. Further, if the route measure units are miles and there is accuracy to the foot, the lowest precision you should use is 5,280.

Suppose you have a route feature class in which the route measure units are kilometer and the route storage units are accurate to the meter level. Further suppose that this route feature class has an m domain in which the measure minimum is -1,000 and the measure precision is 100, which is incorrect. If a new route is created in this feature class and its measure values are set to range between 0 and 1,324.526, the following diagram illustrates that the accuracy of the route's measures is not maintained when the route is stored and subsequently retrieved from the geodatabase. Note that the same process happens for every measure value on the route.

If the route feature class has an appropriate m precision of 1,000, the measure accuracy of the route is maintained on a round-trip to the geodatabase.

When an incorrect measure precision is used, measure accuracy can be lost on a round-trip to the geodatabase.

When a correct measure precision is used, measure accuracy is maintained on a round-trip to the geodatabase.

It is often a good idea to use a precision that is greater than the calculated value to allow for the future storage of more accurate data. In most cases this is not a problem, but be aware that there is a trade-off between precision and the range of measure in which values can be stored. The higher the precision value that is used, the smaller the range of measure values that routes can have.

Grid size

Another consideration regarding geodatabase feature classes is the grid size of the spatial index. The spatial index is used to quickly locate features that match the criteria of a spatial search.

For most data, only a single grid size is required. Because feature size is an important factor in determining an optimum grid size, data that contains features of very different sizes may require additional grid sizes so larger features can be queried faster. Feature classes in ArcSDE geodatabases may have up to three grid sizes. Each grid size must be at least three times the previous grid size. For a more detailed discussion of spatial indexes and grid sizes, see the ArcSDE Administration Guide PDF file and the ArcSDE Configuration and Tuning Guide for <DBMS> PDF file.

When creating a new route feature class, the default grid size is 1,000. This value should be changed. When merging lines to create routes, calibrating route measures with points, or migrating route data to a geodatabase, the default grid size is in the units of the input coordinate system. If you change the output coordinate system, you need to set a new grid size so it is in the units of the output coordinate system. For example, if the input feature class has a geographic coordinate system and its units are decimal degrees, the default grid size may be 10. If the output coordinate system is set to be UTM meters, the default grid size should be set to a value suitable for new units, such as 10,000.

If an inappropriate grid size is used, an error stating that the grid size is too small may occur when storing features into a feature class, or you may experience poor spatial search performance.

Creating route feature classes

You create new route feature classes in ArcCatalog. When creating a route feature class, you must define the geometry field's geometry type to be polyline and indicate that it be able to store measure values. You also need to add a route identifier field. This field uniquely identifies each route.

When creating a route feature class in a geodatabase, you must also define the spatial reference. Note that if you are creating a feature class in a preexisting feature dataset, you need only set the m domain. This is because all feature classes in a feature dataset share a common spatial reference, which was created when the feature dataset was created. The m domain, however, can be different for each feature class. This is because route feature classes in a feature dataset often have different units of measure—for example, feet, meters, and miles.

When creating a shapefile that will store routes, you may choose to define the coordinate system later. It will be classified as Unknown until that time. ▶

Creating a new standalone feature class to store routes

1. Right-click the geodatabase, in the Catalog tree, in which you want to create a new route feature class, point to New, then click Feature Class.

2. Type a name for the new feature class. To create an alias for this feature class, type the alias.

3. Click Next. ▶

The process of defining a shapefile's attributes is separate from creating the shapefile itself. To create the route identifier plus all other fields, you need to right-click in the Catalog tree and click Properties to define the attributes. Note that because a shapefile must contain at least one field, the integer field Id has already been added. Add the appropriate fields to the shapefile, then delete the default field.

Tip

Using another feature class as a template

When creating a new feature class in a geodatabase, you can use another feature class as a template. Click Import, navigate to the feature class whose field definitions you want to copy, then click OK. You can edit the field names and types as required.

See Also

For details about using configuration keywords with ArcSDE, see the ArcSDE Configuration and Tuning Guide for <DBMS> PDF file.

If your geodatabase does not use ArcSDE, skip to Step 5.

4. Click Use configuration keyword and click the keyword you want to use if you want to create a feature class with a custom storage keyword.

5. Click Next.

6. Click the SHAPE field in the Field Name column.

7. Click the field next to Alias and type the alias to create an alias for the SHAPE field.

8. Click the field next to Allow NULL values, click the dropdown arrow, then click No to prevent null shapes from being stored.

9. Click the field next to Geometry Type, click the dropdown arrow, then click Line for the feature's type.

10. Click the fields next to the grids and type the grid value to set the spatial index grid parameters for the feature class.

11. Click the field next to Contains M values, click the dropdown arrow, then click Yes.

12. Click the Spatial Reference Properties button. ▶

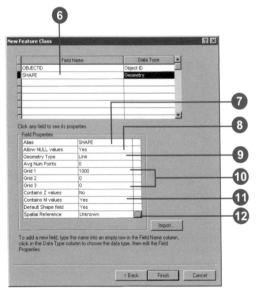

Precision

The size of a spatial domain (XY, Z, or M) is dependent on the value of precision. When the precision is changed, the maximum value for the domain will change to fit the size of the extent. Similarly, when the maximum value is changed, the precision will change to fit the extent.

See Also

For details on how to create a new coordinate system and for important information about spatial references and how they affect your data, see Building a Geodatabase.

13. Click Select, Import, or New to set the feature class's coordinate system.

14. Click the X/Y Domain tab.

15. Type the Min X, Min Y, and Precision values for the XY Domain.

16. Click the M Domain tab.

17. Type the Min, Max, and Precision values for the M Domain.

18. Click OK. ▶

Creating a route feature class in an existing feature dataset

The process of creating a route feature class in an existing feature dataset is similar to that of creating a standalone route feature class. Steps 13 through 15 of 'Creating a new standalone feature class to store routes' are not valid because all feature classes in a feature dataset share a common spatial reference, which was created when the feature dataset was created and cannot be changed. The exception is the m domain, which you should always set.

Creating an index on the route identifier field

It is recommended that you create an attribute index on the route identifier field. This index will improve dynamic segmentation performance.

For more information on creating a field index in a feature class, see Building a Geodatabase.

For more information on creating a feature class in a feature dataset, see Building a Geodatabase.

19. Add the route identifier field to the feature class.

    Click in the next blank row in the Field Name column and type a name.

20. Click in the Data Type column next to the new field's name and click its data type.

21. Either click the property in the dropdown list or type the property to set other properties specific to the type of field.

22. Repeat steps 19 through 21 until all the feature class's fields have been defined.

23. Click Finish.

See Also

For more information on creating shapefiles, see Using ArcCatalog.

Creating a new shapefile to store routes

1. Right-click the folder, in the Catalog tree, in which you want to create a new shapefile, point to New, then click Shapefile.

2. Type a name for the new shapefile.

3. Click the Feature Type dropdown arrow and click Polyline.

4. Check Coordinates will contain M values.

5. Click Edit to define the shapefile's coordinate system.

   When you are finished setting the shapefile's coordinate system (Step 7), you will be returned to this dialog box. ▶

Creating an index on the route identifier field

It is recommended that you create an attribute index on the route identifier field. This index will improve dynamic segmentation performance.

See Also

For more information on creating a field index in a shapefile, see Using ArcCatalog.

6. Click Select, Import, or New to set the shapefile's spatial reference.

7. Click OK.

8. Click OK.

9. Add the route identifier field to the feature class. Right-click the feature class in the Catalog tree and click Properties. ▶

Deleting the default Id field

The integer field Id is a default field and can be deleted once another field has been added to the shapefile.

10. Click the Fields tab.

11. Click the next blank row in the Field Name column and type in a name of the route identifier field.

12. Click in the Data Type column next to the new field's name and click its data type.

13. Click in the Field Properties list and type the properties for the new field.

14. Repeat steps 9 through 12 until all the shapefile's fields have been defined.

15. Click OK.

Creating routes from existing lines

You create routes from existing lines in ArcToolbox. Input linear features that share a common identifier are merged to create a single route.

The input feature classes can be any supported format. This includes coverage, shapefile, personal and enterprise geodatabase, and CAD data.

As the input linear features are merged, the route measures are determined in one of three ways:

- The geometric lengths of the input features are used to accumulate the measures.

- A value stored in a measure field is used to accumulate the measures.

- The values stored in from- and to-measure fields are used to set the measures.

With the first two options, you choose whether the output routes will have continuous measures when there are disjointed parts. ▶

1. Navigate to the Linear Referencing toolbox in the Toolbox tree and double-click Create Routes Wizard.

2. Navigate to the input feature class or type in the name and location of the input feature class.

3. Click the Route Identifier Field dropdown arrow and click the route identifier field.

4. Click Next.

5. Click how you want the output route measures to be obtained.

6. Uncheck Ignore spatial gaps if you do not want spatial gaps to be ignored when measures are being set.

   This option will not be available if you chose Use two fields from the input feature class in Step 5.

7. Click Next.

   If you chose Use two fields from the input feature class in Step 5, skip to Step 10. ▶

ArcInfo and ArcEditor

Also with the first two options, you control the direction measures are assigned to the routes by specifying the coordinate priority of the starting measure. The coordinate priority can be upper left, upper right, lower left, or lower right. These options are determined by placing the minimum bounding rectangle around the input features that are going to be merged to create one route.

It is possible to specify a query to limit the number of linear features that are used to create routes.

The output routes can be written to a shapefile or a geodatabase feature class.

If your input features have a defined projection, the Create Routes Wizard will preserve this projection. You can choose to change the projection information for the output, in which case the features will automatically be projected. Note that you cannot change the projection if you are writing to an existing feature dataset.

When writing to a geodatabase, you should always set the m domain. A default m domain will be calculated for you, but this might not accurately reflect your data. ▶

8. Click the coordinate priority appropriate for your data.

9. Click Next.

10. Click where you want to write the output route feature class.

11. Click Next.

   If you chose Shapefile, skip to Step 25.

12. Navigate to the database or database connection into which you want to write the new route feature class, or type its name and location.

13. Click the dropdown arrow and click the feature dataset to which you want to migrate if you want to migrate to an existing or new feature dataset.

   Type the name of the new feature dataset if you want to migrate to a new feature dataset.

   Leave it blank if you want to migrate to a standalone feature class.

14. Type a name for the new feature class.

15. Click Change Settings.

   When finished setting the feature class's coordinate system (Step 24), you will return to this dialog box. ▶

When writing to a geodatabase, you should examine the grid size for the output spatial index. If your input route feature class is already in a geodatabase, the suggested grid size will be the same as the input. In all other cases, a default will be approximated.

16. Click Change.

17. Click Select, Import, or New if you want to change the output coordinate system.

    These are not available when migrating to an existing feature dataset.

18. Click the X/Y Domain tab if you wish to change the Min X, Min Y, and Precision values for the XY Domain.

    This is not possible when creating a feature class in an existing feature dataset. ▶

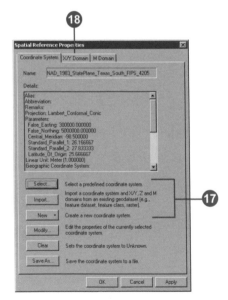

ArcInfo and ArcEditor

Tip

Precision

The size of a spatial domain (XY, Z or M) is dependent on the value of precision. When the precision is changed, the maximum value for the domain will change to fit the size of the extent. Similarly, when the maximum value is changed, the precision will change to fit the extent.

19. Click the M Domain tab.

20. Type the Min, Max, and Precision values for the M Domain.

21. Click OK.

22. Click the Grid Size tab and type the grid size or sizes if you want to set the spatial index grid parameters for the feature class.

    Only one index grid is used in personal geodatabases, while ArcSDE geodatabases use up to three. ▶

For more information about configuration keywords with ArcSDE, see the ArcSDE Configuration and Tuning Guide for <DBMS> PDF file.

If your geodatabase does not use ArcSDE, skip to Step 25.

23. Click the Config Keyword tab, click Use configuration keyword, then type the keyword you want to use if you want to create a feature class with a custom storage keyword.

24. Click OK.

Skip to Step 26.

25. Navigate to the folder into which you want to write the new shapefile or type its name and location.

26. Click Next. ▶

27. Click whether you want to use all features or only those features that satisfy a query.

28. Click Next.

29. Review your settings and click Finish.

Calibrating routes with points

You calibrate routes with points in ArcToolbox. When calibrating, you can choose to exclude routes without any associated calibration points from the output.

The calibration of whole or partial routes is possible.

Route measures can be updated using the shortest path distance between the calibration points or using the existing measure distance between the points. In most applications, using the shortest path distance between the calibration points will be sufficient. Calibrating by measure distance should be used on data for which the length to measure ratio is not consistent at various locations along the input routes.

When calibrating using the shortest path distance, you can choose whether the output routes will have continuous measures when there are disjointed parts.

A tolerance can be specified to limit how far a calibration point can be from a route. Points outside the tolerance will not be used by the calibration process. The tolerance is expressed ▶

1. Navigate to the Linear Referencing toolbox in the Toolbox tree and double-click Calibrate Routes Wizard.

2. Navigate to the route feature class, or type in the name and location of the route feature class.

3. Click Exclude features with no calibration points from the output feature class if applicable.

4. Click the Route Identifier Field dropdown arrow and click the route identifier field.

5. Click Next.

6. Navigate to the point feature class, or type in the name and location of the point feature class.

7. Click the Point Identifier field dropdown arrow and click the point identifier field.

8. Click the Measure field dropdown arrow and click the measure field.

9. Type a tolerance.

10. Click Next. ▶

ArcInfo and ArcEditor

in the same units as the route feature class's coordinate system.

It is possible to calibrate linear features without existing measures. In this situation, the input linear features will be merged (if necessary) based on the route identifier field before the calibration process begins. This initial step is not performed if the input features already have measure values.

The input feature classes can be any supported format. This includes coverage, shapefile, personal and enterprise geodatabase, and CAD data.

It is possible to specify a query to limit the number of points that are used to calibrate.

The output routes can be written to a shapefile or a geodatabase feature class.

If your input route features have a defined projection, the Calibrate Routes Wizard will preserve this projection. You can choose to change the projection information for the output, in which case the features will automatically be projected. Note that you cannot change the projection if you are writing to an existing feature dataset. ▶

11. Uncheck any interpolation or extrapolation options you do not want. They are all checked by default.

12. Click the calibration method you want to use.

13. Uncheck Ignore spatial gaps if you do not want gaps ignored.

14. Click Next.

15. Click where you want to write the output route feature class.

    If you chose Shapefile, skip to Step 30.

16. Click Next.

17. Navigate to the database or database connection into which you want to write the new route feature class, or type its name and location.

18. Click the dropdown arrow and click the feature dataset if you want to migrate to an existing feature dataset.

    Type the name of the new feature dataset if you want to migrate to a new feature dataset.

    Leave it blank if you want to migrate to a standalone feature class.

19. Type a name for the new feature class.

20. Click Change Settings. ▶

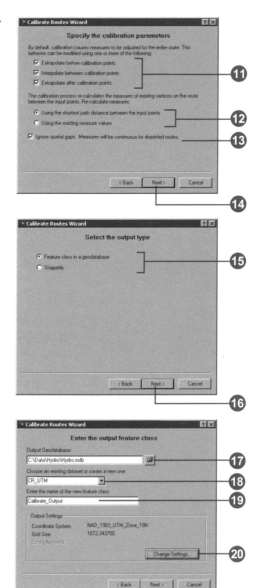

If your input points have a projection different from the routes, they will be projected to that of the routes before the calibration process begins.

When writing to a geodatabase, you should always set the m domain. A default m domain will be calculated for you, but this might not accurately reflect your data.

See Also

For details on how to create a new coordinate system and for important information about spatial references and how they affect your data, see Building a Geodatabase.

21. Click Change.

22. Click Select, Import, or New if you want to change the output coordinate system.

    These are not available when migrating to an existing feature dataset.

23. Click the XY Domain tab if you wish to change the Min X, Min Y, and Precision values for the XY Domain.

    This is not possible when creating a feature class in an existing feature dataset. ▶

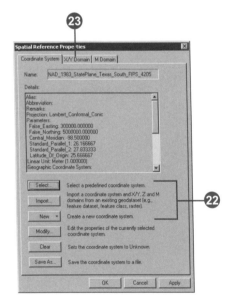

ArcInfo and ArcEditor

Tip

Calibrate Routes Wizard

You can add the Calibrate Routes Wizard to ArcCatalog context menu choices.

See Also

For more information on adding a command to a context menu, see Using ArcCatalog.

24. Click the M Domain tab.

25. Type the Min, Max, and Precision values for the M Domain.

26. Click the Grid Size tab and type the grid size or sizes if you want to set the spatial index grid parameters for the feature class.

Only one index grid is used in personal geodatabases, while ArcSDE geodatabases use up to three. ►

For more information about configuration keywords with ArcSDE, see the ArcSDE Configuration and Tuning Guide for <DBMS> PDF file.

If your geodatabase does not use ArcSDE, skip to Step 29.

27. Click the Config Keyword tab, click Use configuration keyword, then type the keyword you want to use if you want to create a feature class with a custom storage keyword.

28. Click OK.

Skip to Step 30.

29. Navigate to the folder into which you want to write the new shapefile or type its name and location.

30. Click Next. ▶

31. Click whether you want to use only the point features that satisfy a query.

32. Click Next.

33. Review your settings and click Finish.

Migrating route data to a geodatabase

ArcCatalog and ArcToolbox each contain tools to migrate route data from one supported format to another. During the conversion, all measure values are preserved. The example in this section converts a coverage route system to a geodatabase feature class.

When migrating to a geodatabase, you can create a standalone feature class, a feature class in a new feature dataset, or a feature class in an existing dataset.

If your input route features have a defined projection, the data conversion tools will preserve this projection. You can choose to change the projection information for the output, in which case the features will automatically be projected. Note that you cannot change the projection if you are writing to an existing feature dataset. ▶

Tip

Coverage to Geodatabase
The Coverage to Geodatabase tool is also available in ArcToolbox.

Migrating a coverage route system to a geodatabase

1. Right-click the coverage route system, in the Catalog tree, that you want to migrate, point to Export, then click Coverage to Geodatabase.

2. Navigate to the database or database connection to which you want to migrate, or type its name and location.

3. Click the dropdown arrow and click the feature dataset to which you want to migrate if you want to migrate to an existing or new feature dataset.

   Type the name of the new feature dataset if you want to migrate to a new feature dataset.

   Leave it blank if you want to migrate to a standalone feature class.

4. Type a name for the new feature class.

5. Click Change Settings.

   When you are finished setting the spatial reference (Step 13), you will be returned to this dialog box. ▶

A default m domain will be calculated for you. If your source feature class is a coverage or shapefile, you should consider changing the default. This is because the default is calculated by simply expanding the minimum and maximum measure values from the input by some factor. This can result in an m domain with a precision value that is artificially high. A high precision limits the range of measure values that can be stored in the future.

The data conversion tools will suggest a default grid size for the output spatial index. This suggested grid size is only an approximation.

See Also

For more information on migrating existing data to a geodatabase, see Building a Geodatabase.

6. Click Change.

7. Click Select, Import, or New if you want to change the output coordinate system.

   This is not possible when migrating to an existing feature dataset.

8. Click the X/Y Domain tab if you wish to change the Min X, Min Y, and Precision values for the XY Domain.

   This is not possible when migrating to an existing feature dataset. ▶

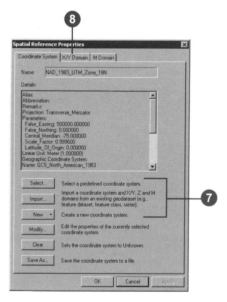

9. Click the M Domain tab.

10. Type the Min, Max, and Precision values for the M Domain.

11. Click the Grid size tab and type the grid size or sizes if you want to set the spatial index grid parameters for the feature class.

   Only one index grid is used in personal geodatabases, while ArcSDE geodatabases use up to three. ▶

Tip

Corrected field names

Different databases allow different field names. The data conversion tools automatically make any necessary changes. You can review these changes and choose to accept them or assign your own names.

See Also

For more information on data mapping, see Building a Geodatabase.

See Also

For more information about configuration keywords with ArcSDE, see the ArcSDE Configuration and Tuning Guide for <DBMS> PDF file.

12. Click the Item names tab if you want to review or change the field mappings.

Make any necessary changes to the Corrected Fields and Delete Field columns.

If your geodatabase does not use ArcSDE, skip to Step 14.

13. Click the Keyword tab, click Use configuration keyword, then type the keyword you want to use if you want to create a feature class with a custom storage keyword.

14. Click OK.

15. Click OK.

Displaying and querying routes and events

5

IN THIS CHAPTER

- **The route identifier field**

- **Querying route data**

- **Hatching**

- **Displaying hatches**

- **Manipulating the text on hatches**

- **Hatch styles**

- **Route measure anomalies**

- **Dynamic segmentation**

- **Adding route events**

Geographic data is represented on a map as a *layer*. Route and event data is no different. ArcMap provides you with the tools to add route and event data to a map as a layer. ArcMap also provides you with many tools for symbolizing and labeling route and event layers in a wide variety of ways.

Once your route and event data have been added to a map, you can gain much insight by just looking at it. You may, however, want to discover spatial relationships that are not apparent to the naked eye. ArcMap provides you with a number of tools to find answers to questions such as Where is...?, What is...?, Where is the closest...?, What's inside...?, and What intersects...? In addition to these tools, ArcMap provides you with tools designed specifically for linear referencing data. With these additional tools, you can:

- Find route and measure information by pointing at your map.

- Find route locations on a map by providing route and measure information.

For more information on displaying and querying your data, refer to *Using ArcMap*.

The route identifier field

ArcMap is aware when data has been added to the map. When route data is added, ArcMap exposes some extra properties for the new layer. One of these new properties is the route identifier field.

The *route identifier* uniquely identifies each route within a feature class. The route identifier field can be any numeric or character field in your route feature class.

Setting the route identifier field saves steps when using many of the linear referencing and dynamic segmentation dialog boxes and wizards in ArcMap.

Tip

Saving the route identifier field

If the layer is saved as a layer file (.lyr), the route identifier field is saved as well.

Setting the route identifier field

1. Right-click the layer, in the table of contents, that you want to set the route identifier field for and click Properties.

2. Click the Routes tab.

3. Click the Route Identifier dropdown arrow and click the field that is to be used as the route identifier.

4. Click OK.

Querying route data

A lot of information can be derived from a map by just looking at it. There are times, however, when you need to know more. Because of this, ArcMap provides you with the tools for querying your maps in a wide variety of ways. In addition to the standard suite of map query tools, you can also find and identify route locations.

See Also

For more information on querying maps or adding commands to a toolbar or menu, see Using ArcMap.

Adding the Identify Route Locations tool

1. Click Customize from the ArcMap Tools menu.

2. Click the Commands tab.

3. Click Linear Referencing in the Categories list.

4. Drag the Identify Route Locations tool to the toolbar of your choice (e.g., the Tools toolbar).

5. Click Close.

Tip

The Identify Route Locations tool is not enabled

The Identify Route Locations tool will not be enabled when there are no route layers in the map.

Tip

Route Identifier field

The values displayed on the branches of the route locations tree correspond to the values in the Route Identifier field. See 'Setting the route identifier field' in this chapter.

Tip

Layer dropdown list

Use the Layer dropdown list to identify route locations from specific layers only.

Identifying route locations

1. Click the Identify Route Locations tool.

2. Click the map in which you want route and measure information.

Labeling an identified route location with a text graphic

1. Right-click on a found route location and click Label route location.

Route identifier field

The Find dialog box pays attention to the route identifier field. If you have not set the route identifier field, then you will need to click the Route Identifier dropdown arrow and click the field to be used for the route identifier between Steps 3 and 4. See 'Setting the route identifier field' in this chapter.

Finding a route location

1. Click the Find tool on the ArcMap Tools toolbar.

2. Click the Route Locations tab.

3. Click the Route Reference dropdown arrow and click the layer that is the route reference.

4. Optionally, click the Load Routes button.

5. Click the Route dropdown arrow and click the route.

   Alternatively, type the route identifier in the Route dropdown list.

6. Click whether the route location will be point or line.

7. Type the route measure information.

8. Click Find.

9. Right-click the found route location and explore the context choices available to you.

Hatching

Hatching is a type of labeling that is designed to post and label hatch marks or symbols at a regular interval along measured linear features. Hatching can be used for both distance-based and nondistance-based measures. Distance-based measures include kilometers, miles, feet, and meters. Nondistance-based measures include seismic shot point numbers where measure values generally increase in even intervals based on some nominal distance.

Hatching can be used in applications with either distance-based or nondistance-based measures.

Hatching concepts

To display hatches on a layer, you must define one or more *hatch classes* for the features you wish to hatch. Each hatch class is composed of one or more hatch definitions.

The easiest way to understand hatch classes and hatch definitions is to use a ruler analogy. On a ruler, there is a series of vertical lines, or hatches, separated by a regular interval. For example, on a centimeter (cm) ruler, the hatches are typically spaced every millimeter (mm). One millimeter is 1/10 of a centimeter, so the hatch interval is 0.1.

Not all the hatches on a ruler are the same. Some are longer than others. Further, some have text, while others do not. On a centimeter ruler, the hatches placed at every millimeter (0.1 cm) are the shortest. The hatches placed at every 5 millimeters

(0.5 cm) are a bit longer. The hatches placed every 10 millimeters (1 cm) are the longest. The longest hatches typically have text to indicate the measure value.

In this example, the ruler is a hatch class. It is a container for the hatch definitions. There are three hatch definitions. Each definition is placed at a multiple of the hatch interval. The longest hatches are placed at every 0.1 x 10 measure units. The second longest hatches are placed at every 0.1 x 5 measure units. The shortest hatches are placed at every 0.1 x 1 measure units.

In this example, the ruler represents a hatch class. The interval of the hatches is 0.1 cm (1 mm). There are three hatch definitions. Each definition is placed at a multiple of the hatch interval—10, 5, and 1, respectively. Some hatch definitions are labeled, while others are not.

When placed on a map, hatch definitions within a single hatch class will not draw on top of one another.

There is a special type of hatch definition known as an *end hatch definition*. An end hatch definition pays no attention to the specified hatch interval. Rather, it simply draws hatch marks at the low and high measure of a linear feature. For cases in which hatches get placed too close together near the end of a feature, it is possible to specify an end hatch tolerance, which prevents certain hatches from drawing if they are within the tolerance (specified in measure units) of an end hatch.

Imagine that you have linear features whose measures are in miles. You want to place a hatch every quarter of a mile. This is a hatch interval of 0.25. Further, you want the hatches placed at every 0.25, 0.5, and 1 mile to look different (different length, different color). You want the hatches every mile to have text. Lastly, you want hatches at the ends of the feature. These end hatches are to look different than all other hatches and will have text. The following example demonstrates conceptually how hatching works in this scenario.

How hatching works

In this example, the line is 4 miles long, and the hatch interval is 0.25. To make hatches look like the following, four hatch definitions are necessary.

— HatchDef(1) - placed every 0.25 miles (0.25 x 1). Does not have text.

— HatchDef(2) - placed every 0.5 miles (0.25 x 2). Does not have text.

— 1 HatchDef(4) - placed every 1 mile (0.25 x 4). Has text.

— 0.0 HatchDef(End) - placed only at route ends. Has text.

Step 1: The hatch definition with the highest multiple of the hatch interval - HatchDef(4) - is placed first. Because an end hatch definition has been specified, no hatches are placed at the ends even though the measure values are divisible by the hatch interval.

Step 2: The hatch definition with the next highest multiple of the hatch interval - HatchDef(2) - is placed. These hatches will not overwrite hatches that have already been placed.

Step 3: The hatch definition with the next highest multiple of the hatch interval - HatchDef(1) - is placed. These hatches will not overwrite hatches that have already been placed.

Step 4: The end hatch definition - HatchDef(End) - will be placed.

Hatching options

There are many ways in which you can control how hatches appear on a map. The following illustrate some of the ways hatches can be manipulated.

All of the hatch definitions in a hatch class can be offset by the same amount. Alternately, each individual hatch definition can have its own offset.

Each hatch definition can be displayed to the left, centered on, or to the right of a feature. When set to center, hatches will be labeled to the left of the feature.

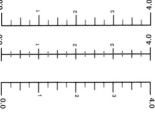

Hatching can start at a measure location other than the low measure. Further, hatching can finish at a location other than the high measure.

In the case in which a feature's geometry has multiple parts, it is possible to apply hatches to the feature as a whole or to each part individually.

By default, the placement of hatches is adjusted to the hatch interval. This means that in cases in which a line's low measure is not divisible by the interval, the first hatch will be placed at the first

measure value that is divisible by the hatch interval. For example, a line whose measures range from 1.1 to 5.2 will have its first hatch placed at 1.25 when the hatch interval is 0.25. This behavior can be turned off. Note that end hatch definitions are not affected by this setting and are not shown in this example.

In cases in which a feature's high measure is not divisible by the hatch interval and an end hatch definition has been defined, it is possible to get

two hatches that are very close to or on top of one another. To avoid this, it is possible to specify an end hatch tolerance, which informs the hatching algorithm to not place hatches when they fall within the tolerance of the end hatch. The end hatch tolerance is specified in route measure units, and its value is typically set to a value that is less than the hatch interval.

Hatches are drawn perpendicular to the feature. It is possible to specify a supplemental angle that is added to the calculated angle.

Hatch text is flipped as the direction of the feature changes. This is to make the text more readable. This can be turned off so the text is always oriented in the direction of increasing measure.

Hatches can also be placed only at the route ends. In this case, it is not necessary to specify a hatch interval.

Creating and managing hatches

Hatches are a feature layer property. As such, hatches are created and managed on the Layer Properties dialog box.

The Hatches tab on the Layer Properties dialog box has three views: the hatch class view, the hatch definition view, and the end hatch definition view. The hatch class view is enabled when a hatch class is selected in the hatch tree. The hatch definition view is enabled when a hatch definition is selected in the hatch tree. The end hatch definition view is enabled when an end hatch definition is selected in the hatch tree.

Hatch Class view

Note that a hatch class is highlighted in the hatch tree.

The Hatch tab is only available for linear feature layers with measures.

The preview indicates what the hatches in the currently selected hatch class will look like.

Hatch classes and hatch definitions can be defined but not visible.

Each hatch class can be visible or not visible. This is useful when more than one hatch class has been defined.

A hatch class always has at least one hatch definition.

Right-clicking on a hatch class in the tree displays a context menu.

Hatches can be imported from another layer in the map document or from a layer file (.lyr).

A single hatch interval can be applied to all features, or different hatch intervals can be stored in a field. The hatch interval is always specified in the same units as the route measures.

A hatch style can be applied to the selected hatch class.

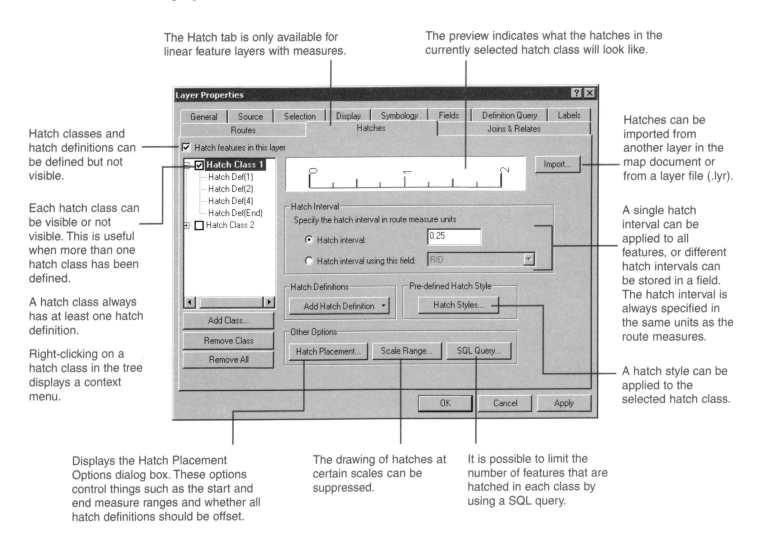

Displays the Hatch Placement Options dialog box. These options control things such as the start and end measure ranges and whether all hatch definitions should be offset.

The drawing of hatches at certain scales can be suppressed.

It is possible to limit the number of features that are hatched in each class by using a SQL query.

Hatch Definition view

Note that a hatch definition is highlighted in the hatch tree.

The selected hatch definition is highlighted using the ArcMap selection color.

A hatch definition is placed at a multiple of the hatch interval. The hatch interval is set on the Hatch Class view.

A hatch definition can be symbolized with either a line or marker symbol.

A hatch definition's name includes the multiple of the hatch interval at which the hatches are to be placed.

No two definitions within the same class can have the same multiple of the hatch interval.

Right-clicking on a hatch definition in the tree displays a context menu.

The line length and lateral offset properties are specified in the units that are set on the Hatch Placement Options dialog box.

Displays the Hatch Orientation dialog box.

Displays the Label Settings dialog box.

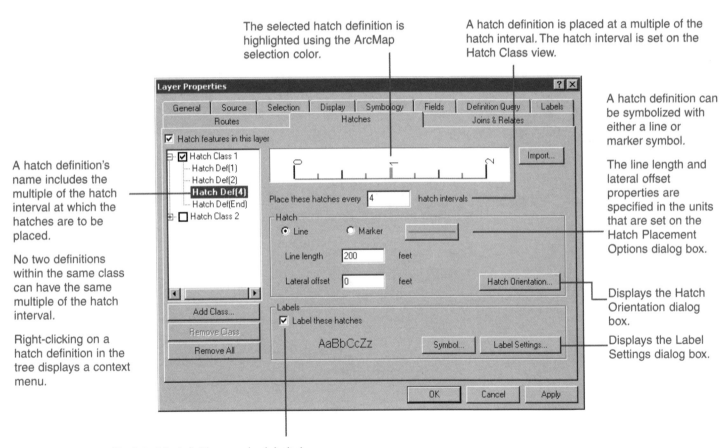

Each hatch definition can be labeled with the route measure.

End Hatch Definition view

Note that an end hatch definition is highlighted in the hatch tree.

The selected end hatch definition is highlighted using ArcMap selection color.

An end hatch definition is a special type of hatch definition. These hatches are only placed at the line ends.

Right-clicking on an end hatch definition in the tree displays a context menu.

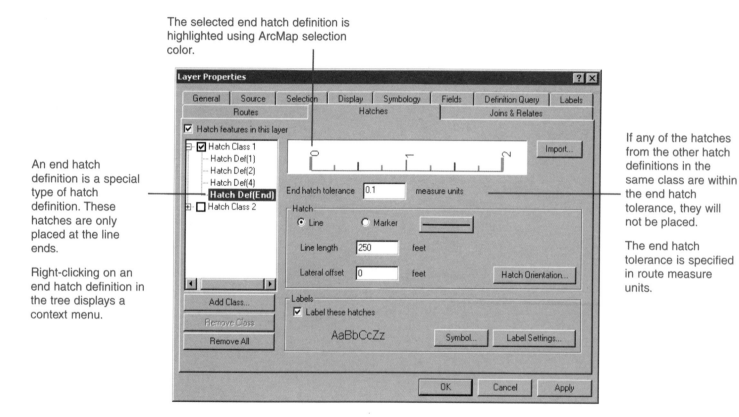

If any of the hatches from the other hatch definitions in the same class are within the end hatch tolerance, they will not be placed.

The end hatch tolerance is specified in route measure units.

Hatch Placement Options dialog box

This dialog box is initiated by clicking the Hatch Placement button on the Hatch Class view. The settings made on this dialog box apply to all the hatch definitions that make up the selected hatch class.

The distance units apply to offsets and hatch definition lengths. They do not refer in any way to the hatch interval, which is specified in route measure units.

The default distance units are the same as the active data frame's display units.

It is possible to start hatching at a value other than the lowest measure. A single value can be applied to all features, or different values can be stored in a field. These values are always specified in route measure units.

In some cases, the low measure of a line is not exactly divisible by the hatch interval. The first hatch placed will be adjusted to a measure value that is divisible by the hatch interval. This behavior can be turned off.

All hatch definitions in a class can be offset by a value. A single offset can be applied to all features, or different offsets can be stored in a field.

Note that it is possible to offset individual hatch definitions. This is done on the hatch definition view.

It is possible to finish hatching at a value other than the highest measure. A single value can be applied to all features, or different values can be stored in a field. These values are always specified in route measure units.

In some cases, a line might have multiple parts. It is possible to apply all hatch settings to each part individually.

Hatch Orientation dialog box

This dialog box is initiated by clicking the Hatch Orientation button on the Hatch Definition view. The settings made on this dialog box apply only to the currently selected hatch definition.

The default is to draw line hatches perpendicular to the line.

A hatch definition can be drawn to the left, right, or center of the line. Text is placed on the left side for the center option.

Label Settings dialog box

This dialog box is initiated by clicking the Label Settings button on the Hatch Definition view. The settings made on this dialog box apply only to the currently selected hatch definition.

The default is to flip the text as the direction of the line changes.

The default is to plot the negative sign for negative measure values.

By default, a hatch's text will only be the measure.

Alternatively, a prefix and/or a suffix can be plotted before the measure values.

Lastly, label expressions can be built using VBScript or JavaScript.

The precision of the value is displayed for the hatch's text. The measure value will be rounded off to the precision specified.

This option is not available when a text expression is being used.

Displaying hatches

Hatches are line or marker symbols displayed on top of features at an interval specified in route measure units. Hatches allow you to make maps that are suitable for almost any application that uses measured linear features.

Layers based on linear features with measures always have at least one hatch class associated with them. Initially, the default hatch class contains one hatch definition. Additional hatch definitions can be added to this hatch class. Each hatch definition has its own set of properties. These include the multiple of the hatch interval at which the hatches in the hatch definition will be placed, the line or marker symbol of the hatches, and whether the hatches will be labeled. The use of multiple hatch definitions allows you to design complex hatching schemes.

Because hatch definitions might share many of the same properties, it is possible to copy the properties of a hatch definition and change only the properties that are different.

Any number of hatch classes can be associated with a layer. ▶

Hatching features in a layer

1. Right-click the layer in the table of contents that you want to hatch and click Properties.

2. Click the Hatches tab.

3. Check Hatch features in this layer.

4. Type an appropriate hatch interval.

5. Click Hatch Def(1).

   The Hatch Definition view becomes active.

6. Type an appropriate line length. ▶

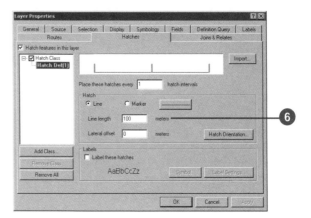

Each hatch class can contain any number of hatch definitions. One reason to create multiple hatch classes is to hatch some features one way and other features another way. To do this, you would associate a SQL query with your hatch classes. Another reason to have multiple classes is to have hatches appear differently at different scales. To do this, you would specify a scale range with your hatch classes.

In situations when you need hatches at the end of features, you need to add an end hatch definition to the hatch class.

To appear on a map, hatches must be turned on via a check box. Note that it is possible to turn each individual class on or off as well.

To save time, it is possible to import hatches from another layer. These layers may be in the map or may have been stored on disk as a layer file (.lyr). Note that if any of the hatch properties in the layer you are trying to import from are based on a field (e.g., the hatch interval), then that field must exist in the layer you are trying to import to.

Another time-saving method is the use of hatch styles. For more information on hatch styles, see 'Hatch styles' in this chapter. ▸

7. Right-click the hatch class and click Add Hatch Definition.

   The Hatch Definition view becomes active.

8. Type an appropriate multiple of the hatch interval.

9. Type an appropriate line length.

10. Check Label these hatches. ▸

Hatches do not respect the ArcMap overposting environment. As such, hatches and their labels can overlap one another. To avoid this, specifying a different hatch interval often alleviates the problem. In some situations, however, it is desirable to convert hatches to graphics so they can be moved on the map.

Tip

Hatches do not appear on the map

If hatches do not appear after you have set up your hatch classes and hatch definitions, make sure that (1) the Hatch features in this layer box is checked, (2) the box beside each hatch class in the tree is checked, (3) the specified hatch interval is appropriate for the data, and (4) all hatch definitions that use a line symbol have an appropriate line length specified.

Tip

Stopping the drawing process

If you selected a hatch interval that is too small, too many hatches will be drawn to the screen. The drawing process can be stopped by pressing the Esc key.

11. Right-click the hatch class and click Add End Hatch Definition.

    The End Hatch Definition view becomes active.

12. Type an appropriate end hatch tolerance if necessary.

13. Type an appropriate line length.

14. Check Label these hatches.

15. Click OK.

Making hatches and their labels bigger when you zoom in

As you zoom in and out on your map, the sizes of the hatches and their labels do not change. If you want the hatches and text to scale with the map, set a reference scale. Right-click the data frame and click Set Reference Scale.

Importing hatches from another layer

1. Right-click the layer in the table of contents that you want to hatch and click Properties.

2. Click the Hatches tab.

3. Click Import.

4. Click the Layer dropdown arrow and click the layer you want to import hatches from.

   Alternately, click the Browse button and navigate to the layer file (.lyr) that you want to import hatches from.

5. Click OK.

6. Click OK.

Tip

**Removing hatch classes
and hatch definitions**

*The currently selected hatch class
or hatch definition can be removed
by right-clicking and clicking
Remove or by pressing the Delete
key.*

Copying a hatch definition's properties

1. Right-click the hatch definition that you want to define the properties for and click Copy Properties From.

2. Click the hatch definition dropdown arrow and click the hatch definition whose properties you want to copy.

3. Click OK.

Adding the Convert Hatches to Graphics command

1. Click Customize from the ArcMap Tools menu.

2. Click the Toolbars tab.

3. Check Context Menus in the Toolbars list.

   The Context Menus toolbar appears. ▶

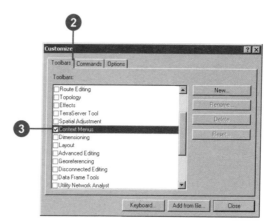

See Also

For more information on adding commands to a toolbar or menu, see Using ArcMap.

4. Click the Context Menus dropdown list and click Feature Layer Context Menu.

5. Click the Commands tab.

6. Click Linear Referencing in the Categories list.

7. Click the Save in dropdown arrow and click where you want your customization saved.

8. Drag the Convert Hatches To Graphics command to the Feature Layer Context Menu.

9. Click Close.

Converting hatches to graphics

1. Right-click the layer in the table of contents whose hatches you want to convert to graphics and click Convert Hatches To Graphics.

2. Click the features for which you want to create graphics.

3. Uncheck any hatch classes you do not want converted to graphics if appropriate.

4. Click the Target annotation group dropdown arrow and click the annotation target where you want to add the graphics.

   Alternately, type the name of a new target annotation group.

5. Click OK.

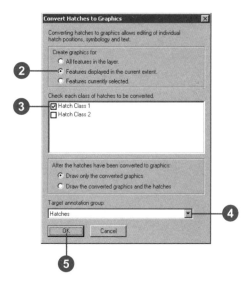

Manipulating the text on hatches

Every hatch definition may or may not be labeled. When labeled, you have control over things such as the text symbol that is used and whether or not the text will automatically be flipped as the direction of the route changes.

By default, the text associated with a hatch is the route measure at the hatch location. This text can be supplemented with a prefix and/or suffix value.

For more advanced needs, you can programmatically generate a hatch's text by writing a script in Microsoft® VBScript™ or JavaScript™. Your script can include any valid statements those programming languages support.

When writing a script, you access the route measure for each hatch using the *esri__measure* constant value.

The script used in the following example tells the hatching algorithm not to label a hatch if its measure value is within 0.1 measure units of the value stored in a field named MMAX. This method can be used instead of an end hatch tolerance, which tells the hatch algorithm not to draw either the hatch or its label.

Generating the text on hatches using a script

1. Right-click the layer in the table of contents that you want to hatch and click Properties.

2. Click the Hatches tab.

3. Follow Steps 3 through 14 of 'Hatching features in a layer' if necessary.

4. Click the hatch definition of your choice.

5. Make sure the Label these hatches check box is checked.

6. Click Label Settings.

7. Click Build a text expression.

8. Click Expression. ▶

For more information on VBScript and/or JavaScript, click the Help button on the Hatch Text Expression dialog box.

9. Check Advanced.

10. Type a VBScript or JavaScript expression.

    ArcMap automatically creates a FindLabel function in your code. FindLabel should evaluate to a string.

11. Click Verify to make sure there are no syntax errors.

12. Click OK.

13. Click OK.

14. Click OK.

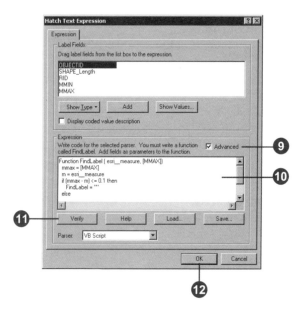

```
Function FindLabel (esri__measure, [MMAX])
   mmax = [MMAX]
   m = esri__measure
   if (mmax - m) <= 0.1 then
      FindLabel = ""
   else
      FindLabel = cstr(round(m,2))
   end if
End Function
```

Hatch styles

A *hatch style* stores the symbols and the settings of the hatch definitions that make up a hatch class. Hatch styles help you maintain standards for displaying your hatches on multiple maps with multiple data sources.

When setting up hatch styles, it is important to note that some of the properties available when setting up a hatch class are not available when setting up a hatch style. These are the properties that are based on attributes, such as class level offsets, start measures, and finish measures.

Like any other style in ArcMap, hatch styles are stored in a style file (.style). Unlike other styles, however, there are no industry-standard hatch styles that come with ArcMap. It is up to you to create your own hatch styles.

Whether you are creating a new hatch style from scratch or altering the properties of an existing one, you use the Style Manager dialog box to work with hatch styles.

See Also

For more information on styles, see Using ArcMap.

Creating a new hatch style in the Style Manager

1. Point to Styles from the ArcMap Tools menu and click Style Manager.

2. Click the Hatches folder in the style tree in the ESRI style file (.style) in which you want to create a new hatch style.

3. Right-click in the open space in the Style contents window, point to New, and click Hatch.

4. Set the style's properties on the Hatch Style properties dialog box and click OK.

5. Name the new hatch style.

Saving a hatch class as a hatch style

1. Click the hatch class that you want to save as a hatch style.

2. Click Hatch Styles.

3. Click Save.

4. Type the name of the new hatch style.

5. Click OK.

6. Click OK.

7. Click Apply.

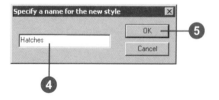

Tip

Applying a hatch style

If you apply a hatch style to a hatch class that already has some hatch definitions in addition to the default definition, they will be overwritten by the hatch definitions in the hatch style.

Applying a hatch style to a hatch class

1. Click the hatch class to which you want to apply a hatch style.

2. Click Hatch Styles.

3. Click the hatch style you want to use.

4. Click OK.

5. Click Apply.

Route measure anomalies

The ArcGIS system does not place any constraints on route measures. Route measures can always increase with respect to a route's digitized direction, always decrease with respect to a route's digitized direction, or be some combination of increasing and decreasing values. Lastly, route measures may be unknown (NaN).

Route measure anomalies are portions of routes where the measures do not conform to the standards your application expects. With the ability to display what you deem to be route measure anomalies in ArcMap, you can ensure that the measures on your routes conform to the needs of your application. Seeing where route measure anomalies occur can help you isolate routes that may need to have their measures edited.

Tip

Scale ranges and SQL queries
Use a scale range and/or a SQL query to control how route measure anomalies are displayed.

Displaying route measure anomalies

1. Right-click the route layer in the table of contents that you want to display route measure anomalies for and click Properties.

2. Click the Routes tab.

3. Click the route measure anomalies you want to display and change the symbology as necessary.

Dynamic segmentation

Geographic data is represented on a map as a layer. Route events are no different. To display route events on a map, however, you must first define the parameters of the relationship between the table storing the events and the routes that the events reference.

Dynamic segmentation (DynSeg) is the process of computing the map location (shape) of events stored in an event table. Dynamic segmentation is what allows multiple sets of attributes to be associated with any portion of a linear feature.

The result of the dynamic segmentation process is a dynamic feature class known as a route event source. A route event source can serve as the data source of a feature layer in ArcMap.

For the most part, a dynamic feature layer behaves like any other feature layer. It is possible to decide whether or not to display it, the scale at which it should be visible, what features or subset of features to display, how to draw the features, whether to store it as a layer file (.lyr), whether to export it, and so on.

A route event source can be edited in ArcMap. It is important to note, however, that it is possible to only edit the attributes. The shapes of a route event source, however, cannot be edited because they are generated by the dynamic segmentation process. When you edit a route event, you are actually editing the underlying event table. As such, there may be some editing limitations imposed by the event table. For example, it is not possible to directly edit the attributes of a route event source created from a delimited text file table since ArcMap does not allow text files to be edited directly.

Advanced dynamic segmentation options

Point events as multipoint features

When a point event is located along a route, a point feature is created. In some applications, however, route measures are not unique. For these applications, it might be desirable to have point events treated as multipoint features.

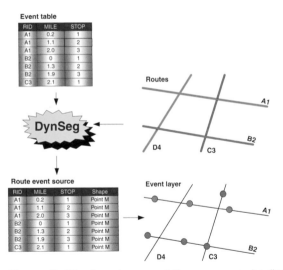

The result of the dynamic segmentation process can be displayed on a map as a layer.

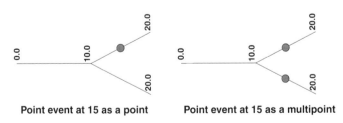

Point events can be located along routes as point features or multipoint features.

Event locating angles

When a point event is located along a route, it is often desirable to know the angle of the route where the event is placed. For example, you might need to rotate the marker symbol that is used to display the event so it is oriented to the route and not the map. Further, you might need to rotate a point event's label.

The dynamic segmentation process can calculate either the normal (perpendicular) or tangent angle. Further, it is possible to calculate the complement of these angles so you can, for example, control the side of the route on which a rotated label appears.

The dynamic segmentation process can calculate the angle of a route at a point event's location.

Event locating errors

The dynamic segmentation process creates a shape for each row in the input route event table. In some cases, however, the shape of the event feature might be empty. This happens when there was some reason that the event could not be properly located. In other cases, an event can only be partially located; this happens for line events only.

The dynamic segmentation process can expose the locating error, if any, for each event in an event table as a field. This field is useful when performing quality assurance tests on your event tables.

RID	MILE	LOC_ERROR
A1	4.5	NO ERROR
A1	12.7	NO ERROR
A1	16.2	ROUTE MEASURE NOT FOUND
B2	0	ROUTE NOT FOUND
B2	1.3	ROUTE NOT FOUND

RID	FMP	TMP	LOC_ERROR
A1	5.5	11.0	NO ERROR
A1	13.1	17.0	PARTIAL MATCH FOR THE TO-MEASURE
B2	16.2	3	ROUTE NOT FOUND

The dynamic segmentation process is aware of the locating status of each event. This information can be exposed as a field.

Event offsets

In some applications, events with an offset are to be drawn to the right of the route. In other applications, events with an offset are to be drawn to the left. The dynamic segmentation process allows you to control which side of the route events with offsets is drawn.

Adding route events

A *route location* describes a portion of a route or a single location along a route. When route locations are stored in tables, they are known as *route events*. Route event tables are typically organized around a common theme. For example, an event table for highways might include speed limits, year of resurfacing, present condition, and accidents.

There are two types of route events: point and line. Point ▶

Tip

Route identifier field
The Add Route Events dialog box will pay attention to a route layer's route identifier field.

Tip

Attribute indexes
Dynamic segmentation performance is improved with the use of an attribute index on the route identifier field in both the event table and the route reference.

Tip

Displaying route events
Right-click on an event table in the Table of Contents and click Display Route Events.

1. Click Add Route Events from the ArcMap Tools menu.

2. Click the Route Reference dropdown arrow and click the route reference layer.

   Alternately, click the Browse button and navigate to the route reference feature class.

3. Click the Route Identifier dropdown arrow and click the route identifier field if necessary.

4. Click the Event Table dropdown arrow and click the event table.

   Alternately, click the Browse button and navigate to the event table.

5. Click the Route Identifier dropdown arrow and click the route identifier.

6. Click the type of events the route event table contains.

7. For point events, click the Measure dropdown arrow and click the Measure field.

   For line events, click the From-Measure dropdown arrow and click the from-measure field. Click the To-Measure dropdown arrow and click the to-measure field.

8. Optionally, click the Offset dropdown arrow and click the offset field.

9. Click Advanced Options. ▶

events occur at precise locations along a route. Line events describe a portion of a route.

A route event table has at least two fields: a route identifier and one or two measure locations. The route identifier indicates the route the event is located along. The measure location is either one or two values describing the positions on the route where the event occurs.

The process of computing the map location of events stored in an event table is known as dynamic segmentation.

The result of the dynamic segmentation process is a route event source, which can be used by a layer in a map.

Tip

Layer files

You save event layers as a layer file (.lyr). The next time you bring this file into ArcMap, the dynamic segmentation process will automatically be performed for you.

Tip

Advanced options

It is possible to have the advanced dynamic segmentation options applied to subsequent ArcMap sessions.

10. Click all of the advanced dynamic segmentations you want applied to the route event source.

11. Click OK.

12. Click OK.

Editing routes

6

IN THIS CHAPTER

- **Adding the Route Editing toolbar**

- **Creating routes from existing lines**

- **Calibrating routes with points**

- **Route measures**

- **Remeasuring routes**

In addition to the display and query of routes and events, ArcMap is the application for creating and editing route features in your spatial database. ArcMap has tools for editing routes that are stored in shapefiles or geodatabase feature classes.

When editing routes, it is important to remember that you are simply editing linear features. If you already know how to edit linear features, you already know how to edit routes. The one thing that differentiates the editing of routes from other linear features is the presence of measure values stored with the feature's vertices. Hence, the editing of route features can be thought of as two distinct processes. The first is the editing of the route's geometry. The second is the editing of the route's measures.

This chapter shows you how to edit routes and route measures in ArcMap. Route editing requires prior knowledge of editing linear features in ArcMap. It is assumed that you already have a good understanding of how to edit linear features in ArcMap. For more information, see *Editing in ArcMap*.

ArcInfo and ArcEditor

Adding the Route Editing toolbar

Before you edit your route data in ArcMap, you need to add the Route Editing toolbar.

Tip

Adding the Editor toolbar
You should also ensure that the Editor toolbar has been added. To do this, click the Editor Toolbar button *on the ArcMap Standard toolbar.*

Tip

Adding the Route Editing toolbar using the Editor menu
From the Editor menu on the ArcMap Editor toolbar, point to More Editing Tools and click Route Editing.

Tip

Adding the Route Editing toolbar using the Customize dialog box
From the ArcMap Tools menu, click Customize, click the Toolbars tab, then click Route Editing.

1. Point to Toolbars from the ArcMap View menu and click Route Editing.

2. Click the toolbar's title bar and drag it to the ArcMap application window.

Creating routes from existing lines

ArcMap provides a variety of tools for creating linear features. Because a route is simply a linear feature with measures, if you are already familiar with the various techniques for creating linear features, you are already familiar with some of the techniques for creating routes.

The following pages outline the steps for creating routes from existing line features. The number of steps differs depending on whether you want to create a simple or complex route. A complex route loops back on itself or branches.

When you create routes from existing lines, you must select the lines whose geometry you want to copy to create the route. The selected features can be from one or more of the linear feature layers already in your map. Further, they can be from any supported data format.

You can use any method available to you to select the linear features. For example, you can use the Edit tool on the Editor toolbar, the Select Features tool on the Tools toolbar, Select by Attributes, and so on. ▶

Creating a simple route

1. Click the Task dropdown arrow and click Create New Feature.

2. Click the Target layer dropdown arrow and click a route layer.

3. Using any available method, select the linear feature or features whose geometry you want to copy to make the route.

   For example, click the Edit tool on the Editor toolbar, move the mouse pointer over a feature, and click the feature. Press the Shift key and continue to click all the features you want to use to create the route.

   The selected features will be highlighted.

4. Click the Make Route button. ▶

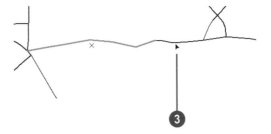

ArcInfo and ArcEditor

Once the linear features have been selected, you will use the Make Route dialog box to set the parameters for how your new route will be created.

The first parameter you set is the start point. This is where the route measure values will begin. There are two ways to set the start point. First, you can click a point on the map. When you choose this option, you will note that as you drag your mouse around the map, the start point automatically snaps to one of the selected feature's endpoints. Second, you can use a coordinate priority of lower left, lower right, upper left, or upper right. These coordinate priorities are determined using the minimum bounding rectangle around the selected set of linear features. The endpoint from the selected features that is closest to the chosen coordinate priority will be where the measures start. ▶

Tip
Cannot see the start point on the map

If you cannot see the start point on the map, it may be because you are not zoomed out far enough to see all of the endpoints of the selected features. Note that you can interact with other ArcMap commands and tools (e.g., Pan, Zoom Out, Zoom to Selected Features) when the Make Route dialog box is displayed.

---

5. Click the Start Point button.

6. Drag your mouse over the selected linear features and click the map when the start point is where you want the route measures to start.

7. Click how you want the route measure values to be obtained.

8. Click Make Route.

   The newly created route is now selected.

The next parameter you set indicates how the measure values are to be obtained. When you choose the geometric length option, it is important to realize that the geometric length of each selected feature is determined in the units of the target layer's coordinate system and not necessarily the feature's native coordinate system. This is to account for the fact that within a single data frame, features with different coordinate systems can be projected on the fly.

The measure field option is only enabled when all the selected linear features are from the same layer. Measure values on the new route will be accumulated using the values in this field.

Use the From/To option when you know the start and end measure values for the new route. All measure values between the start and end will be interpolated for you.

The last parameter you set indicates whether or not you want the measures to be continuous on disjointed routes. Note that if you choose to have noncontinuous measures, the gap distance is calculated using the units of the target layer's coordinate system. This might cause unexpected measure values, for example, when you use a field that stores mileage ▶

Creating a complex (looping) route

1. Click the Task dropdown arrow and click Create New Feature.

2. Click the Target layer dropdown arrow and click a route layer.

3. Using any available method, select a simple chain of linear features that do not form a loop.

   For example, click the Edit tool on the Editor toolbar, move the mouse pointer over a feature, and click the feature. Press the Shift key and continue to click all the features you want to use to create the route.

   The selected features will be highlighted.

4. Click the Make Route command on the Route Editing toolbar. ▶

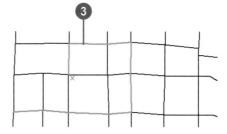

ArcInfo and ArcEditor

values to accumulate the measure and the target layer's coordinate system units are meters. Note that this check box is not available when the From/To option has been chosen to set the measures.

Once the new route has been created in the target feature class, the selected set of input linear features will become unselected, and the new route will become selected. This is so that you can set its attributes, such as the route identifier. For more information on editing attributes, see *Editing in ArcMap*.

The process of creating a complex route is similar to that of creating a simple route. The only real difference is that you must build a complex route in pieces. Once the pieces are created, they can be merged together.

The work flow shown here for creating a complex (looping) route is not the only one. With your knowledge of editing in ▶

Tip
Coordinates or measures out of bounds

If you get the Coordinates or measures out of bounds message when creating a route, it is because the measure values that are being applied to the new route do not fit in the m domain. For more information, see 'Route data' in Chapter 4.

5. Click the Start Point button.

6. Drag your mouse over the selected linear features and click the map when the start point is where you want the route measures to start.

7. Click how you want the route measure values to be obtained.

8. Click Make Route.

   The newly created route is now selected.

9. Using any available method, select a simple chain of linear features that form the second half of the loop.

10. Click the Make Route tool on the Route Editing toolbar. ▶

ArcMap, you may choose a work flow that is more appropriate for your organization.

Take note of the fact that in the complex route example shown here, care has been taken to set the measures appropriately for each of the two halves of the route that is eventually merged together. If this is not possible in your situation, you can still merge the pieces together. Then at a later time, the measure values can be reset. For more information, see 'Remeasuring routes' in this chapter.

11. Click the Start Point button.

12. Drag your mouse over the selected linear features and click the map when the start point is where you want the route measures to start.

13. Click how you want the route measure values to be obtained.

14. Click Make Route.

    The newly created route is now selected.

15. Using any available method, select the two routes that will form the loop. ▶

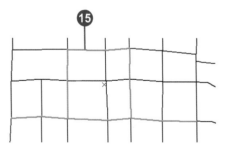

ArcInfo and ArcEditor

Tip

Preserving overlapping segments

The Preserve overlapping segments check box only appears when you are merging two routes. Make sure this box is checked (the default) when you are creating a looping route.

16. Click the Editor menu and click Merge.

17. Click OK.

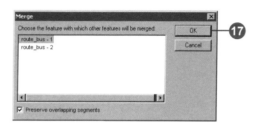

Calibrating routes with points

It is important to have accurate measure values along routes, especially when the measures are used to tie in large amounts of event data.

It is possible to adjust route measures to correspond with known measure locations with a procedure called calibration. *Calibration* adjusts route measures using points. A route can be successfully calibrated with two or more points.

Once you have selected the route that you want to calibrate, you must digitize the points to use for calibration. To digitize the points, you use the Sketch tool. Optionally, you can set the snapping environment. For example, you might want to snap to points that are stored in another feature class. Because one route is calibrated at a time, there is no point-to-route cutoff tolerance specified. All digitized points will be assumed to fall on top of the selected route. ►

Tip

Undo

If you digitize a point you do not like, click the Undo button ↶ *on the ArcMap Standard toolbar.*

1. Click the Task dropdown arrow and click Calibrate Route Feature.

2. Click the Edit tool, move the mouse pointer over a route feature, and click the feature.

3. Click the Calibrate Route tool on the Route Editing toolbar.

   The Calibrate Route dialog box will appear.

4. Click the Sketch tool.

5. Click the map at each location you want a calibration point.

   You will see the Calibrate Route dialog box's point list being populated as you click the points. ►

Once all the calibration points have been digitized, you must then type the new measure value for each point.

Either whole or partial routes can be calibrated. You can choose to interpolate between the calibration points, extrapolate before the calibration points, extrapolate after the calibration points, or use any combination of these methods.

In order for the measure value on a vertex to be interpolated or extrapolated, a calibration ratio is needed. There are two ways this ratio can be determined. The first method uses the shortest path distance between the input points. The second method uses the existing measure distance between the input points.

When calibrating disjointed routes, you may choose to ignore the distance of the spatial gap between the parts. If you choose to ignore spatial gaps, route measures will be continuous. If you want the spatial gap incorporated in the measures, the gap distance is the straight-line distance between the endpoints of the parts.

Tip

Order is important

Make sure you digitize the calibration points in either route increasing or decreasing order, rather than in some random order.

6. Type the new measure value for each clicked point.

7. Click the calibration options you would like.

8. Click Calibrate Route.

Route measures

Editing existing routes

Whenever a route's geometry is edited in ArcMap, its measure values are edited as well. Because of this, there are three rules that are followed whenever a route's geometry is changed.

First, the measure value on newly added vertices is interpolated when the new vertex falls between two vertices with known measure values.

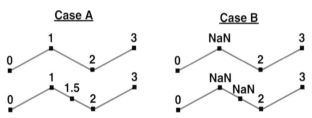

A new vertex will have its measure value interpolated only when it is created between two vertices that have known measure values.

Second, in cases where a route's geometry has been extended, newly added vertices will not have their measure value extrapolated.

A new vertex will not have its measure value extrapolated when a route is extended.

Finally, certain editing commands, such as Merge, Union, and Intersect, take two or more input geometries and produce an output geometry. In some cases, these commands will encounter situations where the input geometries overlap. Consequently, these commands must choose which of the input feature's measures to use in the output. In such cases, the measure values from the feature that was selected first will be used.

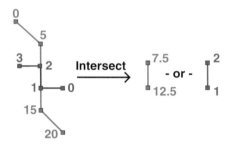

When geometries overlap, some editing commands must choose which of the input feature's measures will be used for the output. In these cases, the measures from the feature that was selected first will be used. In this intersect example, both possible results are shown.

Setting route measures

The following methods can be used to set a route's measure values. It is possible to apply all of these methods to whole or partial routes.

Set As Distance—Set the route's measure values to be the cumulative length from the origin of the geometry. Hence, route measures will increase with the digitized direction of the route.

Set measures as the distance from the route's origin.

ArcInfo and ArcEditor

Set From/To—Set the route's measures using known start and end values. All measure values between the start and end will be interpolated.

In some applications, the ratio between a route's length and its measures is not constant. When the Set From/To method is applied to a route, it is possible to preserve the measure schema that exists. That is, this method can assign measure values based on the original measure value.

Do not preserve existing measure schema

Preserve existing measure schema

Set the start measure to be 0 and the end measure to be 100. All measure values in between are interpolated.

Sometimes a constant change needs to be applied to a route's measures. This is the case whenever measures need to be rescaled or converted into different units or simply incremented by some value. You can meet these needs by using the next two methods.

Apply Factor—Multiply a route's measures by a factor.

Multiply route measures by a factor of 10.

Offset—Add a value to a route's measures.

Offset route measures by 5.

Calculate NaN—Interpolate or extrapolate all route measures that are unknown (NaN).

Interpolate or extrapolate unknown measure values.

Drop Measures—Set all route measures to NaN.

Set all route measures to NaN.

Set Direction As M—There is no requirement that a route's measures increase with the digitized direction. This method will flip a route's geometry to match the direction in which the measures are increasing.

Set a route's digitized direction to match the direction of the measures.

Remeasuring routes

Route measures need to be edited, for example, when more accurate information has been obtained or when the geometry of the route has been altered in some way.

Route measures are edited via an edit sketch. When editing route measures, the edit sketch is simply a shape that represents a copy of the route's geometry. Once you have made the necessary changes to the route measures, you finish the edit sketch. Finishing the sketch writes the sketch geometry to route. ▶

Tip

Edit Sketch Properties

Because route measures are set on an edit sketch, open the Edit Sketch Properties dialog box ▨ *if you want to see the changes as they happen.*

Tip

Double-clicking to modify a feature

When the Edit tool is selected, you can double-click a feature when you want to modify it. The edit task will automatically change to Modify Feature.

Setting measures as distance

1. Click the Task dropdown arrow and click Modify Feature.

2. Click the Edit tool, move the mouse pointer over the route feature you want to remeasure, and click the feature.

    A copy of the selected route's geometry is written to the edit sketch.

3. Right-click on the edit sketch, point to Route Measure Editing, and click Set As Distance.

4. Type the starting measure value and press Enter.

    At this point, the changes to the measures have been applied to the sketch only. To finish the sketch, press F2 or simply unselect the route feature.

ArcInfo and ArcEditor

Realigning a route is the act of defining a new course for a route. Once a route is realigned, you may need some portions of the route measures to remain unchanged, while other portions need to be updated. Because of this need, it is possible to remeasure whole routes or portions of routes. ▶

Tip

Coordinates or measures out of bounds

If you get the Coordinates or measures out of bounds message when remeasuring a route, it is because the measure values that are being applied to the route do not fit in the m domain.

Tip

Using the Route Measure Editing options multiple times

There are many situations in which you may need to use the Route Measure Editing options more than once to achieve the desired result. For example, you may want the route measures on a new route to be stored in miles. The route feature class, however, has been digitized in feet. An easy solution to this is to first use the Set As Distance option to set the measures in feet. Then the Apply Factor option could be used to convert from feet to miles (the factor would be 0.00018939394).

Setting from/to measures

1. Click the Task dropdown arrow and click Modify Feature.

2. Click the Edit tool, move the mouse pointer over the route feature you want to remeasure, and click the feature.

   A copy of the selected route's geometry is written to the edit sketch.

3. Right-click on the edit sketch, point to Route Measure Editing, and click Set From/To.

4. Type the from and to measure values, click whether you want to preserve the existing measure schema, and press Enter.

   At this point, the changes to the measures have been applied to the sketch only. To finish the sketch, press F2 or simply unselect the route feature.

When you are defining a portion of a route to be remeasured, you are actually creating a sketch whose geometry represents just the defined portion. Once the sketch has been created, you use the Route Measure Editing sketch menu—just like you would if you were remeasuring the entire route.

Context menu

When you are defining a portion of a route, you can right-click on the map to display a context menu. The options on this menu allow you to quickly move to any point along the route.

Map tip text

When defining a portion of a route to be remeasured, the text of the map tip corresponds to the measure value at that point along the selected route.

Number of decimals

The number of decimals displayed when defining the subportion of a route corresponds to the number of decimals setting on the General tab of the Editing Options dialog box.

Remeasuring a portion of a route

1. Click the Task dropdown arrow and click Modify Portion of a Line.

2. Click the Edit tool, move the mouse pointer over the route feature you want to remeasure, and click the feature.

3. Click the Define Line Portion tool.

4. Click a point along the selected route to start defining the portion.

5. Click a second point along the selected route to finish defining the portion.

   An edit sketch is created.

6. Right-click on the edit sketch, point to Route Measure Editing, and click the option you want to use to remeasure the portion.

Creating and editing event data

IN THIS CHAPTER

- Creating and editing event data

- Creating event tables in ArcCatalog

- Overlaying events

- Aggregating events

- Transforming event measures

- Locating points along routes

- Locating polygons along routes

- Editing event tables in ArcMap

7

An *event table* is just like any other table in ArcGIS Desktop; it is a database component that contains a series of rows and columns. In an event table, each row describes a location along a route, and each column represents a particular attribute about the route location. Event tables are stored in any supported format—for example, INFO, Microsoft Access, dBASE, Oracle®, SQL Server™, delimited text files, and those databases accessed via OLE DB providers.

In this chapter, you will learn how to create and edit event data and tables. However, before you start creating and editing event data, note that many organizations already maintain large event databases. Quite often, these databases can be accessed and their tables can be used as events without any modification. Any table that contains route identifier and route measure fields—the route location fields—can be used as an event table.

Event tables are generally created in ArcCatalog. They can also be created in the ArcMap Route Events GeoProcessing Wizard. Once created, ArcMap makes it easy to view and update the attributes of the events in your database.

ArcInfo

Creating and editing event data

Creating event data

In order to be used as an event table, a table must contain route location fields, which are used to find the location of the events along routes.

Event tables can be created in ArcCatalog, where there are tools for creating geodatabase, dBASE, and INFO tables.

Event data can be stored in any supported table. Shown here are geodatabase, text file, INFO, and dBASE tables.

There are some additional techniques that automate the task of event table creation:

- Creating point events by locating point features along routes
- Creating line events by locating polygon features along routes
- Overlaying existing event data to create new line or point events

- Aggregating existing event data using concatenate and dissolve operations
- Transforming route measures from one route reference to another

Overlaying events

In ArcMap, geographic data is represented on a map as a layer. When event data has been added to a map in the form of a layer (see 'Adding route events' in Chapter 5), it can be queried according to feature locations and attributes to solve problems. Further, new spatial relationships can be discovered by asking questions such as Where is...?, Where is the closest...?, and What intersects...? For more information on how to find answers to these types of questions, see *Using ArcMap*.

Overlaying events is another way to create new event data. This process combines two input event tables to create a single output event table. The new table can be used to analyze event data in ways not possible using traditional spatial analysis techniques.

The new event table can contain either the intersection or the union of the input events. The union of the input events splits all linear events at their intersections and writes them to the new event table. The intersection of the input event tables writes only overlapping events to the output event table.

Line-on-line, line-on-point (same as point-on-line), and even point-on-point event overlays can be performed.

Line-on-line overlay

A *line-on-line overlay* involves the overlay of two line event tables to produce a single line event table.

Line-on-line overlay

The example below shows the union of a line event table that stores pavement information and another line event table that stores pavement resurfacing dates. The result can be used, for example, to find the characteristics of the oldest paved sections.

RID	FMP	TMP	CRACK
101	23.5	44.2	50
101	44.2	84.7	30
101	84.7	167.4	80
101	167.4	182.8	95
101	182.8	209.5	45

RID	FMP	TMP	RESURF
101	23.5	44.2	2/5/85
101	44.2	84.7	9/3/87
101	84.7	167.4	4/28/61
101	167.4	182.8	1/21/74

RID	FMP	TMP	CRACK	RESURF
101	3.2	21.1	0	2/5/85
101	23.5	44.2	50	9/3/87
101	44.2	84.7	30	9/3/87
101	84.7	95.5	80	9/3/87
101	21.1	23.5	0	9/3/87
101	95.5	167.4	80	4/28/61
101	167.4	182.8	95	4/28/61
101	182.8	190	45	4/28/61

Unioning two event tables can help expose spatial relationships not evident before the overlay. Here, two line event tables are unioned. The output event table contains all of the input events, which have been split where they intersected.

Line-on-point overlay

A *line-on-point overlay* involves the overlay of a line event table and a point event table. The process produces a single point event table.

The example below shows the intersection of a point event table containing accident locations and a line event table containing pavement information. The result can be used, for example, to analyze pavement characteristics where accidents occurred.

RID	MILE	INJ	ALC
101	25.9	2	0
101	95.6	1	1
101	172.3	1	0
101	180.3	3	1

RID	FMP	TMP	CRACK
101	23.5	44.2	50
101	44.2	84.7	30
101	84.7	167.4	80
101	167.4	182.8	95
101	182.8	209.5	45

RID	MILE	INJ	ALC	CRACK
101	25.9	2	0	50
101	95.6	1	1	80
101	172.3	1	0	95
101	180.3	3	1	95

Intersecting two event tables can help expose spatial relationships not evident before the overlay. Here, a line and a point event table have been intersected.

ArcInfo

Aggregating event data

You aggregate existing event data using *concatenate* and *dissolve* operations. These operations are designed to help maintain the integrity of large event tables.

Both the concatenate and dissolve operations combine event records in tables where there are events on the same route and they have the same value for specified fields. The result is written to a new event table. One difference between the two operations is that concatenate will only combine events in situations where the to-measure of one event matches the from-measure of the next event. Dissolve will combine events when there is measure overlap. Another difference is that the dissolve operation is available for both line and point event tables, while the concatenate operation is available only on line event tables.

You can use concatenate or dissolve to remove redundant information from an event table. For example, if one linear event in a pavement event table has an attribute—concrete—from 0 to 100, and the following event record has an attribute—concrete—from 100 to 125, the two events will be merged into a single event from 0 to 125. Getting rid of redundant event information makes all subsequent operations on the events more efficient.

RID	FMP	TMP	MATERIAL
1	0	100	concrete
1	100	125	concrete
1	125	175	asphalt
1	175	205	asphalt
1	205	215	concrete

RID	FMP	TMP	MATERIAL
1	0	125	concrete
1	125	205	asphalt
1	205	215	concrete

Concatenating or dissolving events can be used to remove redundant information from event tables.

Concatenating and dissolving events

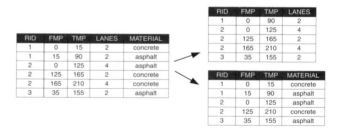

Concatenating and dissolving events combine adjacent records in linear event tables if they are on the same route and have the same values for the dissolve field or fields.

Another use for concatenate or dissolve is to break up event tables having more than one descriptive attribute into separate tables. For example, if a pavement event table has fields LANES and MATERIAL, the event table can be subdivided into two tables: one having the attribute LANES, and the other having the attribute MATERIAL. To do this, the dissolve or concatenate process would need to be run twice.

RID	FMP	TMP	LANES	MATERIAL
1	0	15	2	concrete
1	15	90	2	asphalt
2	0	125	4	asphalt
2	125	165	2	concrete
2	165	210	4	concrete
3	35	155	2	asphalt

RID	FMP	TMP	LANES
1	0	90	2
2	0	125	4
2	125	165	2
2	165	210	4
3	35	155	2

RID	FMP	TMP	MATERIAL
1	0	15	concrete
1	15	90	asphalt
2	0	125	asphalt
2	125	210	concrete
3	35	155	asphalt

Concatenating or dissolving events can also be used to break up event tables with multiple descriptive attributes.

Transforming event measures

In certain circumstances, it may become necessary to update the measure values in an event table. For example:

- Using an event table to reference multiple route references, each of which has its own unit of measure

- Keeping measures up to date when a route is recalibrated or realigned

Use with multiple route references

In many agencies, event data is collected against multiple route reference systems. For example, a DOT might use both a reference marker system and a milepoint system. Some event data, such as accident locations and maintenance activities, is recorded using the reference marker system, while other event data, such as pavement condition or capital improvement projects, is recorded using the milepoint system of measurement.

Every year, a DOT manager is required to determine which sections of highway need to be resurfaced. Using a pavement event table, a manager could determine which segments of pavement have fallen into ill repair. The manager does not, however, want to resurface highways with certain types of accident histories without first performing a safety analysis. The reason for this is that speeds may increase on the new pavement, which could increase the accident rate even further.

In order to make a well-informed decision, it will be necessary to combine and analyze the event data that has been collected against the different route references. The pavement scores are based on milepoint values, while the accident data is based on reference marker system. To combine the event data, the pavement events must be transformed to the reference marker

system, or the accident events must be transformed to the milepoint system.

It is necessary to transform events to analyze events recorded using one route reference with events recorded using another route reference.

In most cases, you will use the ArcMap Route Events GeoProcessing Wizard to transform events from one route reference to another. This wizard calculates the x,y coordinate location of each event in an input route reference and matches this to the corresponding measure values in a second route reference. The structure of the routes need not be the same. A new event table is written out with the events encoded in a different system of measures.

In cases in which route structure is identical and the difference in measures between two reference systems is constant, a simple mathematical equation can be used in lieu of the Route Events GeoProcessing Wizard to transform event measures. For example, if one route reference has its measures in miles and the other has its measures in feet, then all that needs to be done is to multiply the miles by 5,280 in the field calculator to obtain feet.

Keeping event measures up to date

Measure locations tie an event to a particular location along a route. When the measures of a route are altered, the events will no longer be mapped to the same position along their routes.

In some cases, this is the desired result. For example, if the measures along a stream need calibration to match up to known mileages at gauging stations, and the location of fish habitat event data was collected using the gauging stations, then nothing needs to be done to the event data when the route measures are altered.

In other cases, the location of the events when they are mapped must be maintained. For example, if a highway is realigned, the measure of events describing the location of road signs must be updated to maintain their original positions.

Realigning a route causes measure values to change. Events located on this route will no longer be in the same position.

If changes in route measures are linear along the length of a route, an equation can be applied to the event measures. For example, if a route's measures are multiplied by a factor of 1,000 to convert from kilometers to meters, all event measures can also be multiplied by 1,000.

If changes in route measures are nonlinear, such as what happens during a realignment procedure, then the ArcMap Route Events GeoProcessing Wizard can be used to recalculate the measures in an event table to maintain the real-world locations.

Locating point features along routes

When you locate point features along routes, you are determining the route and measure information of where your point data intersects your route data.

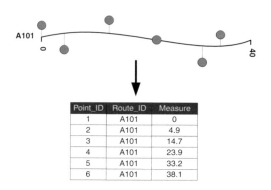

Locating points along routes creates a new point event table containing the route identifier and measure information of where points intersect routes.

Locating point features along routes is useful, for example, when you need to locate:

- Signs along highways
- Wells or gauging stations along river reaches
- Stops along bus routes
- Manholes along city streets
- Valves along pipes

Locating polygon features along routes

Locating polygon features along routes computes the route and measure information at the geometric intersection of polygon data and route data. Once polygon data has been located along routes, the resulting event table can be used, for example, to calculate the length of route that traveled through each polygon.

Poly_ID	Route_ID	From_M	To_M
1	A101	5	16
2	A101	16	24
3	A101	24	38

Locating polygon data along routes computes the geometric intersection of the route and polygon data.

Locating polygon features along routes is useful, for example, when you need to locate:

- Soils, spillways, areas of inundation, or hazard zones along river reaches

- Wetlands, hazard zones, or town boundaries along highways

Editing event data

Event tables are only as good as the information they contain. Over time, you will need to modify event data to keep it accurate and up to date. ArcMap lets you edit event data. You can edit any of the attribute values in an event table as well as add and delete event records. You can also use the field calculator to change the attribute value of a field for several events at once.

Creating event tables in ArcCatalog

You can create geodatabase, dBASE, and INFO event tables in ArcCatalog with easy-to-use table designers.

For a table to be considered an event table, it must contain the appropriate route location fields. For point event tables, the required fields are a route identifier field and a measure field. For line events, the required fields are a route identifier field plus both a from- and a to-measure field. All other fields define each point or line event's attribute information. ▶

Tip

Route location fields

The route identifier field can be any numeric or character data type. You should consider creating an attribute index on the route identifier field; it will help improve dynamic segmentation performance. The measure field or fields must be a numeric data type.

See Also

For more information about creating a table in a geodatabase, see Building a Geodatabase.

Creating a table in a geodatabase

1. Right-click the database in the Catalog tree in which you want to create a new table, point to New, then click Table.

2. Type a name for the table. To create an alias for this table, type the alias.

3. Click Next. ▶

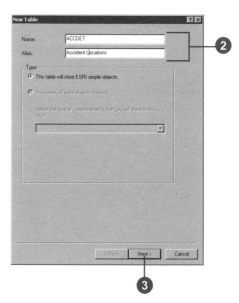

When defining an event table's name and fields, be aware that each database has its own rules defining what names and characters are permitted. Refer to your database's documentation for a list of these rules.

For dBASE tables, the process of defining the attributes is separate from creating the table itself. After creating the table, you need to right-click it in the Catalog tree and click Properties to define the attributes. Because they must contain at least one field, the text field Name1 is added. Add the appropriate fields to the dBASE table, then delete the default field. In a dBASE table, a field name must be 10 characters or less; additional characters will be truncated. ▸

Tip

OBJECTID field in a geodatabase table

The OBJECTID field in a geodatabase table uniquely identifies each object stored in the table. It cannot be deleted.

See Also

For more information about configuration keywords with ArcSDE, see the ArcSDE Configuration and Tuning Guide for <DBMS> PDF file.

If your table does not use ArcSDE, skip to step 6.

4. Click Use configuration keyword and type the keyword if you want to create a table using a custom storage keyword.

5. Click Next.

6. Click the next blank row in the Field Name column and type in a name to add a field to the table.

7. Click in the Data Type column next to the new field's name and click its data type.

8. Click the field next to Alias and type the alias name for this field to create an alias for this field.

9. Click the field next to Allow NULL values and click No to prevent nulls from being stored in this field.

10. Click the field next to Default Value and type the value to associate a default value with this field.

11. Click the field next to Domain and click the domain to associate a domain with this field.

12. Repeat steps 6 through 11 until all the table's fields have been defined.

13. Click Finish.

An INFO table's name must be 32 characters or less, and the item names must be 16 characters or less. Items are defined using standard ArcInfo data types. The input width is the maximum number of characters or bytes used to store the item's values. For numeric items, the width must be large enough to accommodate the decimal point and negative sign. The display width is the number of spaces used to display values in ArcInfo Workstation; for decimal values, the display width should be one space greater than the input width to account for the decimal point.

Tip

OID field in a dBASE table

The OID field in a dBASE table is a virtual field that is created by ArcGIS when the table's contents are accessed. It is used to ensure that each object in the table has at least one unique value. It cannot be deleted.

See Also

For more information about creating a dBASE table, see Using ArcCatalog.

Creating a dBASE table

1. Right-click the folder in the Catalog tree in which you want to create the new table, point to New, then click dBASE Table.

   A new dBASE table appears in the folder's contents.

2. Type the name for the table and press Enter.

3. To add a field to the table, right-click the table in the Catalog and click Properties.

4. Click the Fields tab.

5. Click the next blank row in the Field Name column and type in a name.

6. Click in the Data Type column next to the new field's name and click its data type.

7. Click in the Field Properties list and type the properties for the new field.

8. Repeat Steps 5 through 7 until all the table's fields have been defined.

9. Click OK.

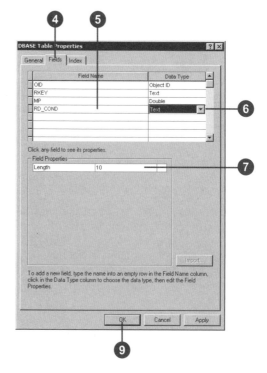

Tip

Creating a new workspace

All INFO files must reside within an INFO workspace. To create a new workspace, right-click on the folder where the workspace will reside in the Catalog tree, point to New, then click ArcInfo Workspace.

See Also

For more information about creating an INFO table, see Using ArcCatalog.

Creating an INFO table

1. Right-click the folder in the Catalog tree in which you want to create the new table, point to New, then click INFO table.

2. Type a name for the new table.

3. Click the data type of the first item in the table.

4. Type the name for the new item.

5. Change the column width, display width, and decimal places as necessary.

6. Click New item to add another item to the table. Then repeat steps 3 through 5 to define the new item's properties.

7. Repeat step 6 until all items have been added to the table.

8. Click OK.

ArcInfo

Overlaying events

You can use the ArcMap Route Events GeoProcessing Wizard to overlay event tables. Line-on-line, line-on-point, and even point-on-point event overlays can be performed.

The event overlay options are only enabled when there are two or more event layers in your map.

To overlay successfully, both the event layers should be based on the same route reference. Otherwise, you may get erroneous results.

The output event table can contain either the intersection or the union of the input events. The union of the input events splits all linear events at their intersections and writes them to the new event table. The intersection of the input event tables writes only overlapping events to the output event table.

If either of the input tables contains point events, the output will always be a point event table.

The new event table can be written to the workspace of your choice. ▶

Overlaying events—Intersect

1. Click the Tools menu and click Route Events GeoProcessing Wizard.

2. Click Intersect two route event layers.

3. Click Next.

4. Click the input route event layer dropdown arrow and click the input event layer.

5. Click the overlay route event layer dropdown arrow and click the overlay event layer.

6. Click Next.

7. Click the Browse button and navigate to a location to save the output event table.

   Alternatively, you can type the name and location of the output event table.

8. Type the names of the output route location fields if you want to change the suggested defaults.

9. Check whether you would like to include all the fields from the input event layers.

10. Check whether you would like the output table added to the map as an event layer, as a standalone table, or not at all.

11. Click Finish.

By default, the output event table contains a route identifier field, the measure fields, plus all of the input event attributes. You can choose to not write out the event attributes. In this case, only the respective event layer's OBJECTID field will be written to the output table. This field can be used at a later time to join or relate back to the original event attributes.

When both inputs are line event tables, you can specify whether you want to keep zero length line events in the output table. These are events where the from- and to-measures are equal and are often created by the overlay process.

You can choose to have the resulting table added to the map as a feature layer, as a standalone table, or not at all.

Tip

Using the selected features

When you overlay events, you can choose whether you want to process only the selected set of features.

Overlaying events— Union

1. Click the Tools menu and click Route Events GeoProcessing Wizard.

2. Click Union two route event layers.

3. Click Next.

4. Click the input route event layer dropdown arrow and click the input event layer.

5. Click the overlay route event layer dropdown arrow and click the overlay event layer.

6. Click Next. ▶

ArcInfo

Tip

Definition queries

When you overlay events, any definition queries set up on the input event layers will be respected.

7. Click the Browse button and navigate to a location to save the output event table.

   Alternatively, you can type the name and location of the output event table.

8. Type the names of the output route location fields if you want to change the suggested defaults.

9. Check whether you would like to include zero length line events in the output table if you are overlaying two line event layers.

10. Check whether you would like to include all the fields from the input event layers.

11. Check whether you would like the output table added to the map as an event layer, as a standalone table, or not at all.

12. Click Finish.

Aggregating events

You can use the ArcMap Route Events GeoProcessing Wizard to aggregate event data. Use the Dissolve/Concatenate route events option to remove redundant information from event tables or to break up event tables having more than one descriptive attribute into separate tables. The result will be written to a new event table in the workspace of your choice. This option is only enabled when there is one or more event layers in your map.

Select concatenate when you want to only combine events in situations in which the to-measure of one event matches the from-measure of the next event. Select dissolve when you want to combine events that have overlapping measures.

You can dissolve or concatenate on one or more fields.

You can choose to have the resulting table added to the map as a feature layer, as a standalone table, or not at all.

Dissolving and concatenating route events

1. Click the Tools menu and click Route Events GeoProcessing Wizard.

2. Click Dissolve/Concatenate route events.

3. Click Next.

4. Click the event layer dropdown arrow and click the event layer to be dissolved/concatenated.

5. Click whether you would like to dissolve or concatenate the events.

   Concatenate will be unavailable if you selected a point event layer in Step 4.

6. Check the box to indicate the attribute or attributes on which to dissolve or concatenate.

7. Click Next. ▶

ArcInfo

Tip

Using the selected features

When you aggregate events, you can choose whether you want to process only the selected set of features.

Tip

Definition queries

When you aggregate events, any definition queries set up on the input event layer will be respected.

8. Click the Browse button and navigate to a location to save the output event table.

   Alternatively, you can type the name and location of the output event table.

9. Type the names of the output route location fields if you want to change the suggested defaults.

10. Click whether you would like the output table added to the map as an event layer, as a standalone table, or not at all.

11. Click Finish.

Transforming event measures

There are two ways you can transform event measures in ArcMap. First, if the required transformation is constant, you can use the field calculator. For example, you can use the field calculator to easily transform event measures between feet and miles.

Second, you can use the Route Events GeoProcessing Wizard's Transform events from one route reference to another option. The wizard will write a new event table to the workspace of your choice. This option is only enabled when there are two or more event layers in your map.

To be transformed successfully, the input events must be within a specified tolerance of the routes in the target route ▶

Tip

Calculating fields outside an edit session
You can calculate field values outside of an edit session. You cannot, however, undo your changes.

See Also

For more information on field calculations, see Using ArcMap.

Transforming event measures using the field calculator

1. Click the Editor menu on the Editor toolbar and click Start Editing if you have not already started an edit session.

2. Open the table you want to start editing.

3. Select the records you want to update. If you don't select any, calculations will be applied to all records.

4. Right-click the field heading for which you want to make a calculation and click Calculate Values.

5. Use the Fields list and Functions list to build a calculation expression. You can also edit the expression in the text area below. Lastly, you can just type in a value to set the field to.

6. Click OK.

reference. The default search tolerance is 0.

The output event table contains all of the input event table's attributes, but the route identifier and measure location information is from the target route reference.

You can choose to have the resulting table added to the map as a feature layer, as a standalone table, or not at all.

Tip

Route structure

When transforming events, the input route structure and target route structure need not be the same.

Tip

Choosing a tolerance

The larger the tolerance you use, the more likely an event will be transformed to the incorrect route in the target route reference. Use as small a tolerance as possible to achieve the best results.

Transforming events using the Route Events GeoProcessing Wizard

1. Click the Tools menu and click Route Events GeoProcessing Wizard.

2. Click Transform events from one route reference to another.

3. Click Next.

4. Click the event layer dropdown arrow and click the event layer to be transformed.

5. Click the Route Reference dropdown arrow and click the target route layer.

6. Click the Route Identifier dropdown arrow and click the route identifier.

   The route identifier uniquely identifies each route.

7. Type the search tolerance, click the dropdown arrow, then click the appropriate units.

   The tolerance defines how far an event can be from a target route in order to be transformed.

8. Click Next. ▶

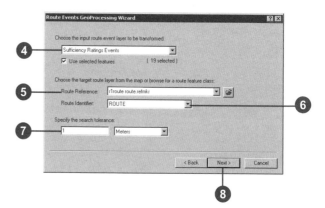

Tip

Using the selected features

When you transform events from one route reference to another, you can choose whether you want to only process the selected set of features.

Tip

Definition queries

When you transform events from one route reference to another, any definition queries set up on the input event layer will be respected.

9. Click the Browse button and navigate to a location to save the output event table.

   Alternatively, you can type the name and location of the output event table.

10. Type the names of the output route location fields if you want to change the suggested defaults.

11. Check whether you would like to include all the fields from the input event layer.

12. Check whether you would like the output table added to the map as an event layer, as a standalone table, or not at all.

13. Click Finish.

ArcInfo

Locating points along routes

You can use the ArcMap Route Events GeoProcessing Wizard to create new point event tables. The Locate point features along routes option finds the route and measure information of either all or a selected set of point features and writes them to a point event table in the workspace of your choice. This option is only enabled when there is one or more point layers in your map.

To be located successfully, the points must be located on or within a specified tolerance of the routes. The default search tolerance is 0. You control the size of the search tolerance by specifying a distance in whichever units you prefer.

By default, the output event table contains the route identifier and measure location of the route on which each point falls, plus all of the attributes from the input point feature class. ▶

Tip

Using a route reference that is not in the map
Use the Browse button to navigate to the location of a route reference that has not been added to the map.

Locating point features along routes

1. Click the Tools menu and click Route Events GeoProcessing Wizard.

2. Click Locate point features along routes.

3. Click Next.

4. Click the point layer dropdown arrow and click the point layer to be located.

5. Click the Route Reference dropdown arrow and click the route layer.

6. Click the Route Identifier dropdown arrow and click the route identifier.

   The route identifier uniquely identifies each route.

7. Type the search tolerance, click the dropdown arrow, then click the appropriate units.

   The tolerance defines how far around each point the search will be done.

8. Click Next. ▶

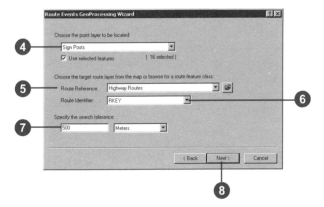

You can choose to not write out the point attributes. In this case only the point's OBJECTID field will be written to the output table. This field can be used at a later time to join or relate back to the original point attributes.

If a point falls within a given search radius of more than one route, you can choose whether only the closest route location or all route locations will be written to the output table.

You can choose to have the resulting table added to the map as a feature layer, as a standalone table, or not at all.

Using the selected features

When you locate points along a route, you can choose whether you want to process only the selected set of point features.

Definition queries

When you locate points along routes, any definition queries set up on the input point layer will be respected.

9. Click the Browse button and navigate to a location to save the output event table.

   Alternatively, you can type the name and location of the output event table.

10. Type the names of the output route location fields if you want to change the suggested defaults.

11. Check whether you would like to include a distance field in the output table.

   The values in the distance field will be in the units specified in Step 7.

12. Check whether you would like to include only the closest route location in the output table.

13. Check whether you would like to include all the fields from the input point layer.

14. Check whether you would like the output table added to the map as an event layer, as a standalone table, or not at all.

15. Click Finish.

ArcInfo

Locating polygons along routes

You can use the ArcMap Route Events GeoProcessing Wizard to create new line event tables. The Locate polygon features along routes option computes the route and measure information at the geometric intersection of polygon data and route data and writes them to a line event table in the workspace of your choice. This option is only enabled when there is one or more polygon layers in your map.

By default, the output event table contains the route identifier and the from- and to-measure information of the route upon which each polygon falls, plus all of the attributes from the input polygon feature class. You can choose to not write out the polygon attributes. In this case, only the polygon's OBJECTID field will be written to the output table. This field can be used at a later time to join or relate back to the original polygon attributes.

You can choose to have the resulting table added to the map as a feature layer, as a standalone table, or not at all.

1. Click the Tools menu and click Route Events GeoProcessing Wizard.

2. Click Locate polygon features along routes.

3. Click Next.

4. Click the polygon layer dropdown arrow and click the polygon layer.

5. Click the Route Reference dropdown arrow and click the route layer.

6. Click the Route Identifier dropdown arrow and click the route identifier.

   The route identifier uniquely identifies each route.

7. Click Next. ▶

Tip

What is a zero length line event?

A zero length line event occurs when the from- and to-measures are the same. This can happen in locating polygons along routes, for example, when a polygon touches a route but does not overlap it.

zero length
line event

Tip

Using the selected features

When you locate polygons along routes, you can choose whether you want to process only the selected set of polygon features.

Tip

Definition queries

When you locate polygons along routes, any definition queries established on the input polygon layer will be respected.

8. Click the Browse button and navigate to a location to save the output event table.

   Alternatively, you can type the name and location of the output event table.

9. Type the names of the output route location fields if you want to change the suggested defaults.

10. Check whether you would like to include zero length line events in the output table.

11. Check whether you would like to include all the fields from the input polygon layer.

12. Check whether you would like the output table added to the map as an event layer, as a standalone table, or not at all.

13. Click Finish.

Editing event tables in ArcMap

You can edit event attributes in two ways: using the event's attribute table or the Attributes dialog box.

As with editing the attributes of any feature, editing event attributes takes place within an *edit session*. You start an edit session by clicking Start Editing from the Editor menu on the Editor toolbar. Once you begin an edit session, you'll notice this icon next to the Options button on the table window, indicating the table can be edited. In addition, ▸

Tip

Adding the Editor toolbar
To display the Editor toolbar, click Tools and click Editor Toolbar.

Tip

Saving your edits often
Click the Editor menu and click Save Edits.

Tip

Dynamic segmentation
When displayed as a feature layer, editing an event's route location field will cause the event's location to be dynamically resegmented.

Editing event records using the table window

1. Click the Editor menu and click Start Editing if you have not started an edit session.

2. Open the event table you want to edit.

   You can open either a standalone event table or one that has been added to ArcMap as a feature layer. For more information, see 'Adding route events' in Chapter 5.

3. Click the cell containing the attribute value you want to change.

4. Type the value and press Enter.

   The table is updated.

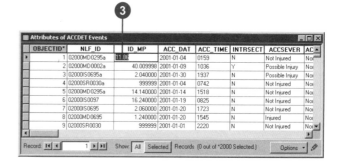

those fields that you can edit will have a white background color for the field heading.

You make attribute changes by clicking a cell and typing a new value. If you make a mistake, you can easily undo the edit by clicking Undo from the Edit menu.

Editing attributes through the table window allows you to quickly make changes to several records at once. When you're editing the attributes of a specific event, you may find it more convenient to use the Attribute dialog box, which is accessed from the Editor toolbar. To use the Attributes dialog box with events, you must first add your events to ArcMap as a feature layer. For more information, see 'Adding route events' in Chapter 5.

The Attributes dialog box has two sides. The left side lists the features you have selected. Features are listed by their primary display field and are grouped by layer name. The right side shows the attribute field names and their values. ▶

See Also

For more information on table editing techniques, such as copying and pasting records and making simple and advanced field calculations, see Using ArcMap.

Adding new event records using the table window

1. Click the Editor menu and click Start Editing if you have not started an edit session.

2. Open the event table you want to edit.

3. Click the arrow on the right to move to the end of the table.

4. Click a cell in the last record and type in a new value.

   Note: If your events table has been added to ArcMap as a feature layer, the new event will appear on the map once valid route location values have been set. For more information, see 'Adding route events' in Chapter 5.

Deleting event records using the table window

1. Click the Editor menu and click Start Editing if you have not started an edit session.

2. Open the event table you want to edit.

3. Select the records you want to delete. Press and hold the Ctrl key while clicking to select more than one record.

4. Press the Delete key on the keyboard.

When you've completed your edits, you can save them and end the edit session.

Tip

Events as a feature layer

For events to be edited with the Attributes dialog box, they must be displayed in ArcMap as a feature layer.

Tip

Noneditable fields

If you are editing your events after they have been added to the map as a feature layer, some fields will not be editable. These are the fields that are generated by the dynamic segmentation process: Shape, Loc_Error, and Loc_Angle.

Tip

Noneditable tables

Some event tables cannot be edited—for example, delimited text files and tables accessed through an OLE DB connection.

Editing event records using the Attributes dialog box

1. Click the Editor menu and click Start Editing if you have not started an edit session.

2. Click the Edit tool.

3. Select the events whose attributes you want to edit.

4. Click the Attributes button.

5. Click the primary display field of the event feature for which you want to modify an attribute value.

6. Click the value you want to modify.

7. Type a new value and press Enter.

   The attribute is modified for the event feature.

See Also

For more information on editing attributes with the Attributes dialog box, see Editing in ArcMap.

Deleting event records using the Attributes dialog box

1. Click the Editor menu and click Start Editing if you have not started an edit session.

2. Click the Edit tool.

3. Select the event you want to delete.

4. Click the Attributes button.

5. Right-click the primary display field of the event feature you want to delete and click Delete.

Glossary

alias

Another name for a field in a table.

attribute

1. A piece of information describing a map feature. The attributes of a route might include its route identifier, its measure length, the day it was built, and so on.

2. A column in a database table.

bookmark

See spatial bookmark.

CAD

See computer-aided design.

calibration

A procedure that recalculates route measures by first setting the measure value at known locations (points) and then interpolating and/or extrapolating all other measure values.

Catalog tree

Contains a set of folder connections in ArcCatalog that provides access to geographic data stored in folders on local disks or shared on a network. It also includes folders that let you manage database connections and coordinate systems. The Catalog tree provides a hierarchical view of the geographic data in those folders.

computer-aided design (CAD)

An automated system for the design, drafting, and display of graphically oriented information. Also known as computer-aided drafting.

concatenate events

Combines event records in tables where there are events on the same route that have the same value for specified fields; concatenate events will only combine events in situations where the to-measure of one event matches the from-measure of the next event. Concatenate events is available for line event tables only.

coordinate system

A method for specifying the location of real-world features on the surface of the earth.

coverage

A file-based vector data storage format for storing the location, shape, and attributes of geographic features. A coverage usually represents a single theme, such as soils, streams, roads, or land use. It is one of the primary vector data storage formats for ArcInfo.

database management system

A set of computer programs for organizing the information in a database. A database management system supports the structuring of the database in a standard format and provides tools for data input, verification, and storage.

dissolve events

Combines event records in tables where there are events on the same route that have the same value for specified fields; dissolve events combines events when there is measure overlap. Dissolve events is available for both line and point event tables.

dynamic segmentation

The process of computing the map location (shape) of events stored in an event table and displaying them on a map. Also known as DynSeg.

edit session

In ArcMap, all editing takes place within an edit session. An edit session begins when you choose Start Editing from the Editor menu and ends when you choose Stop Editing.

Editor toolbar

A set of tools that allows you to create and modify features and their attributes in ArcMap.

end hatch definition

A special type of hatch definition that draws hatch marks only at the low and high measure of a linear feature.

event

See route event.

event overlay

An operation that produces a route event table that is the logical intersection or union of two input route event tables. Event overlay is one way to perform line-on-line, line-on-point, and event point-on-point overlays.

event table

See route event table.

event transform

See transform events.

extrapolation

In the context of linear referencing, this refers to the calculation of measure values on a route beyond where measure values are currently known.

feature

A representation of a real-world object that can be displayed in a layer on a map.

feature class

An object class that stores features and has a field of type geometry.

feature dataset

A collection of feature classes that shares the same spatial reference.

field

A column in a table. Each field contains the values for a single attribute.

geodatabase

An object-oriented geographic database that provides services for managing geographic data. These services include validation rules, relationships, and topological associations. A geodatabase contains feature datasets and is hosted inside a relational database management system.

hatch class

A container for hatch definitions.

hatch style

Stores the symbols and settings of the hatch definitions that make up a hatch class.

hatches

A series of vertical line or marker symbols displayed on top of features at an interval specified in route measure units.

hatching

A type of labeling that is designed to post and label hatch marks or symbols at a regular interval along measured linear features.

index

Created for an attribute or group of attributes in a feature class or table to improve query performance. Feature classes can also have spatial indexes that improve spatial query performance.

interpolation

In the context of linear referencing, refers to the calculation of measure values for a route between two known measure values.

intersect

The topological integration of two spatial datasets that preserves features that fall within the area common to both input datasets. That is, intersect produces the logical AND between the input datasets. Compare with union.

join

The process of attaching tabular data. The join process allows data from a layer or table (the join table) to be appended to a selected table or layer (the target table).

layer

A collection of similar geographic features—such as highways, rivers, lakes, counties, or cities—of a particular area or place for display on a map. A layer references geographic data stored on a data source, such as a shapefile, and defines how to display it. You can create and manage layers as you would any other type of data in your database.

line event

A feature that describes a portion of a route; it uses a from- and to-measure value. Examples include pavement quality, salmon spawning grounds, bus fares, pipe widths, and traffic volumes.

linear feature

A geographic feature represented by a line. A line connects two or more x,y coordinate pairs. Rivers, roads, and electric and telecommunication networks are all linear features.

linear referencing

A simplified method for storing geographic data by using a relative position along an already existing linear feature. Location is given in terms of a known linear feature and a position, or measure, along it. Linear referencing is an intuitive way to associate multiple sets of attributes to portions of linear features.

linear referencing method

A way to identify a location along a route with respect to a known point.

line-on-line overlay

In linear referencing, this involves the overlay of two line event tables to produce a single line event table. The new event table can be the logical intersection or union of the input tables.

line-on-point overlay

In linear referencing, a line-on-point overlay involves the overlay of a line event table and a point event table to produce a single point event table. The new event table can be the logical intersection or union of the input tables.

map

A graphical presentation of geographic information. It contains geographic data and other elements, such as a title, North arrow, legend, and scalebar. You can interactively display and query the geographic data on a map and also prepare a printable map by arranging the map elements around the data in a visually pleasing manner.

Map Tips

Displays onscreen descriptions of map features when you pause the mouse pointer over the feature.

measure

See route measure.

measure location fields

Either one or two fields in a table that describe the position of an event along a route.

NaN

Not a number.

OLE DB provider

Object Linking and Embedding Database provider. Each provider communicates with and retrieves data from a different database, but you can work with data retrieved by any provider in the same way. Typically, providers can only retrieve nonspatial data. However, if an OLE DB provider can retrieve geographic data in OpenGIS format, you can work with that data in ArcInfo.

overlay events

See event overlay.

point event

A feature that occurs at a precise point location along a route; it uses a single measure value. Examples include accident locations along highways, signals along rail lines, bus stops along bus routes, and pumping stations along pipe lines.

point-on-line overlay

See line-on-point overlay.

polyline

A two-dimensional feature representing a line containing one or more line segments—that is, any line defined by three or more points. Line features, such as boundaries, roads, streams, and streets, are usually polylines.

projection

A mathematical formula that transforms feature locations from the earth's curved surface to a map's flat surface. A projected coordinate system employs a projection or transforms locations expressed as latitude and longitude values to x,y coordinates. Projections cause distortions on one or more of these spatial properties: distance, area, shape, and direction.

raster

Represents any data source that uses a grid structure to store geographic information.

river addressing

In hydrology applications, another name for linear referencing. River addressing allows objects, such as field monitoring stations, which collect information about water quality analysis, toxic release inventories, drinking water supplies, flow, and so on, to be located along a river or stream system.

route

Any linear feature, such as a city, street, highway, river, or pipe, that has a unique identifier and a measurement system stored with the geometry.

Route Editing toolbar

A set of tools that allows you to create and modify routes in ArcMap.

route event

A geographic feature occurring along a linear feature (route). There are two event types: line and point. A route event's shape is determined using dynamic segmentation.

route event source

The result of the dynamic segmentation process. A route event source serves an event table as a dynamic feature class. Every row in the table is served as a feature whose shape is calculated when needed. For example, a route event source can act as the basis of a feature layer in ArcMap.

route event table

A table that stores route locations and their attributes. A route event table, at a minimum, consists of a route identifier field and a measure location field (point events) or fields (line events).

route feature class

See route reference.

route identifier

A numeric or character value used to identify a route.

route location

A discrete location along a route (point) or a portion of a route (line). A point route location uses only a single measure value to describe a discrete location along a route. A line route location uses both a from- and to-measure value to describe a portion of a route.

route measure

A location along a route. Typically, a route measure is the distance (in feet, meters, miles, and so on) from the start point of a route. In some cases, however, measure values are nondistance based (e.g., seismic shotpoints).

route measure anomalies

Route measure values that do not adhere to the expected behavior. They can often be fixed with ArcMap route editing tools.

route reference

A collection of routes with a common system of measurement stored in a single feature class (e.g., a set of all highways in a county).

scale

The relationship between the dimensions of features on a map and the geographic objects they represent on the earth, commonly expressed as a fraction or a ratio. A map scale of 1/100,000 or 1:100,000 means that one unit of measure on the map equals 100,000 of the same units on the earth.

selected set

A subset of features in a layer or records in a table. ArcMap provides several ways to select features and records graphically or according to their attributes.

shapefile

A vector data storage format for storing the location, shape, and attributes of geographic features. A shapefile is stored in a set of related files and contains one feature class.

sketch

A shape that represents a feature's geometry. Every existing feature on a map has an alternate form—a sketch. A sketch lets you see exactly how a feature is composed with all vertices and segments of the feature visible. To modify a feature, you must modify its sketch.

snapping environment

The automatic intersecting of disjointed lines or nodes that arise when map data is being digitized or scanned.

spatial bookmark

In ArcMap, identifies a particular geographic location that you want to save and refer to later—for example, a study area.

spatial domain

Describes the range and precision of x,y coordinates and z- and m-values that can be stored in a feature dataset or feature class in a geodatabase.

spatial reference

Describes both the projection and spatial domain for a feature dataset of a feature class in a geodatabase.

SQL

Structured Query Language. A syntax for defining and manipulating data from a relational database. Developed by IBM in the 1970s, it has become an industry standard for query languages in most relational database management systems.

stationing

In the pipeline industry, another name for linear referencing. Stationing allows any point along a pipeline to be uniquely identified.

Structured Query Language

See SQL.

symbol

A graphic pattern used to represent a feature. Many characteristics define symbols, including color, size, and shape of the symbol used.

table

A set of data elements that has a horizontal dimension (rows) and a vertical dimension (columns) in a database. A table has a specified number of columns but can have any number of rows.

topology

The model used to describe how features share geometry. It is also the mechanism for establishing and maintaining topological relationships between features and feature classes. ArcGIS implements topology through a set of validation rules that defines how features share geographic space and a set of editing tools that works with features that share geometry in an integrated fashion.

transform events

An operation that produces a new table by copying and transforming events from one route reference to another. This allows the events to be used with a route reference having different route identifiers and/or measures.

union

The topological integration of two spatial datasets that preserves features that fall within the area common to either input dataset. That is, union produces the logical OR between the input datasets. Compare with intersect.

Universal Transverse Mercator

See UTM.

UTM

Universal Transverse Mercator. A projected coordinate system that divides the world into 60 north and south zones, six degrees wide.

vector

A coordinate-based data structure commonly used to represent linear geographic features. Each linear feature is represented as an ordered list of vertices.

vector model

A representation of the world using points, lines, and areas. Vector models are useful for representing and storing discrete features, such as buildings, pipes, or parcel boundaries.

vertex

A point that joins two segments of a feature.

wizard

A tool that leads a user step by step through an unusually long, difficult, or complex task.

workspace

A container for geographic data. This includes a folder that contains shapefiles, an ArcInfo workspace that contains coverages, a personal geodatabase, or an ArcSDE database connection.

zero length line event

A line event whose from-measure is equal to its to-measure. This can happen, for example, when locating polygons along routes and the polygon touches a route but does not overlap it.

Index

A

Alias
  defined 153
ArcCatalog 47, 48, 70, 73
ArcInfo Workstation 48
ArcSDE
  storing routes 48
ArcToolbox 47, 48, 73
  calibrating routes with points 67
  creating routes from existing lines 61
Attributes 5
  defined 153
  storing multiple sets 42

B

Bookmark. *See* Spatial bookmark

C

CAD (Computer-aided design) 61, 68
  defined 153
  input feature class 11
Calculating route measures with points. *See*
    Calibrating routes
Calibrate Routes Wizard 11, 68, 70
Calibrating routes
  described 50, 67, 117
  digitizing points
    order of 118
    undoing 117
  disjointed routes 51, 118
  using measure distance 51, 67
  using shortest path distance 50, 67
Calibration
  defined 153
Catalog tree
  defined 153
Complex route
  creating 113

Computer-aided design 153. *See* CAD
Concatenate events
  defined 153
  described 128
Convert Hatches to Graphics command
  adding 96
Coordinate priority 48
Coordinate system
  defined 154
  described 43
Coordinates or measures out of bounds 114
Coverage
  defined 154
Coverage route system
  migrating to a geodatabase 73–76
Coverage to Geodatabase tool
  in ArcToolbox 73
Create Routes Wizard 11, 62, 63

D

Data
  organizing
    in ArcCatalog 10
  storing
    as a multipoint feature 40
    as a point feature 40
    as a polygon feature 40
    as a polyline feature 40
Database management system
  defined 154
Decimals
  number displayed 123
Definition queries 140, 143
Display symbol
  changing 20
Dissolve events
  described 128
Dissolve operation
  defined 154

Dynamic segmentation. *See also* Route events
  advanced options 108
  defined 154
  described 40, 105
  using attribute indexes 107

E

Edit session
  defined 154
Edit Sketch Properties 121
Editor toolbar
  adding 110, 148
  defined 154
Edits
  saving 38, 148
End hatch definition
  defined 154
  described 83
  view 88
Event. *See also* Route events
  defined 154
Event data
  aggregating 128
  editing 131
  storing
    in dBASE tables 126
    in geodatabases 126
    in INFO tables 126
    in text files 126
Event layers
  saving 108
Event measures
  transforming 129, 141–142
    with the field calculator 141
  updating 129
Event overlay
  defined 154
Event records
  adding
    using the table window 149

Event records (continued)
  deleting
    using the table window 149
    with the Attributes dialog box 151
  editing
    using the Attributes dialog box 150
    using the table window 148
Event table. *See also* Route event tables
  defined 154
Event transform. *See also* Route events
  defined 154
Events. *See* Route events
Existing routes
  editing 119
Extrapolation
  defined 154

F

Feature class
  defined 154
  described 43
  using as a template 55
Feature dataset
  defined 154
  described 43
  with multiple route feature classes 43
Features
  defined 154
  described 1
  modifying 121
  splitting or merging 41
  storing as relative locations 41
Field names 76
Fields
  calculating 141
  defined 155
  noneditable 150
Folder connection
  creating 10
From/To measures
  setting 122

G

Geodatabase
  defined 155
Geographic data
  modeling 40
Graphics
  saving 98
Grid size 53

H

Hatch class
  associating a SQL query 92
  defined 155
  described 83
  removing 95
  saving as a hatch style 102
  view 86
Hatch definition
  copying 95
  view 87
Hatch Orientation dialog box 90
Hatch Placement Options dialog box 89
Hatch style
  applying to a hatch class 103
  creating in the Style Manager 101
  defined 155
  described 101
  saving 102
Hatch Style dialog box
  accessing 102
Hatches 91–92
  converting to graphics 96, 98
  creating and managing 85
  defined 155
  described 91–92
  displaying 91
  generating text with a script 99
  importing 94
  intervals of 84

Hatches (continued)
  manipulating text 99
  nonappearing 93
  overlapping with labels 93
  scaling with the map 94
  stopping the drawing process 93
Hatching
  defined 155
  described 83
  distance-based measures 83
  nondistance-based measures 83
  options 84

I

Id field
  deleting 60
Identify Route Locations tool
  adding 22, 79
  not enabled 80
Index
  defined 155
Input width
  described 134
Interpolation
  defined 155
Intersect
  defined 155
  events. *See* Overlay events

J

Join
  defined 155

L

Label Settings dialog box 90
Layer
  defined 155
  described 77

Layer dropdown list
  using 80
Line event
  defined 155
  described 44
  displaying on a map 28. *See also* Dynamic
    segmentation
Line-on-line overlay
  defined 156. *See also* Overlay events
Line-on-point overlay
  defined 156. *See also* Overlay events
Linear feature
  defined 155
  described 39
Linear referencing 45
  defined 155
  described 39
  highways and streets 2
  oil and gas exploration 5
  pipelines 6
  railways 4
  transit 3
  water resources 7
Linear referencing method
  defined 156
  described 45

M

M domain
  choosing 52
Make Route command
  described 34, 112
Map
  defined 156
Map document
  existing
    opening 19
Map Tips
  defined 156
  remeasuring portion of a line 123

Measure distance. *See* Calibrating routes
Measure location fields
  defined 156
Measures. *See also* Route measures
  defined 156
  described 40, 43
  out of bounds 114
  setting as distance 121
  unknown (NaN) 43

N

NaN
  calculating 120
  defined 156
  described 43

O

OBJECTID field 133, 137
OID field 134
OLE DB provider
  defined 156
Overlapping segments
  preserving 116
Overlay events. *See also* Route events
  defined 156
  line-on-line 126
  line-on-point 127

P

Point events
  defined 156
  described 44
  displaying on a map 27. *See also* Dynamic
    segmentation
Point features
  locating along routes 130, 144–145
Point-on-line overlay
  defined 156

Polygon features
    locating along routes 131, 146–147
Polyline
    defined 156
    described 43
    storing a measurement system 43
    with multiple, connected paths 43
    with multiple, disjointed paths 43
    with one path 43
Precision 56, 64
Projection
    defined 156

R

Raster
    defined 157
Reference scale
    setting 94
Route data
    adding to a map 20, 32
    calibrating 15
    creating 11
        measure values are known 49
        measure values are not known 48
    migrating
        to a geodatabase 73–74
    querying 79
Route Editing toolbar
    adding
        using the Customize dialog box 110
        using the Editor menu 110
    defined 157
Route event. *See also* Route events
    defined 157
Route event source
    defined 157
Route event tables
    automated techniques 126
    concatenating 128

Route event tables (continued)
    creating
        in a geodatabase 132–133
        in ArcCatalog 132–133
        in dBASE 134
        in INFO 135
    defined 157
    described 44, 125
    dissolving 128
    editing in ArcMap 148–149
    intersecting 127
Route events
    adding to a map 107. *See also* Dynamic
        segmentation
    aggregating 139
    described 44, 107
    displaying 107
    dissolving and concatenating 139–140
    editing 148
    overlaying 136–137
        intersect 136
        union 137–138
    querying 29
    transforming 142–143
Route Events GeoProcessing Wizard
    aggregating events 139. *See also* Dissolve
        events, Concatenate events
    locating points along routes 144–145. *See*
        also Point features
    locating polygons along routes 146–147. *See*
        also Polygon features
    overlay events 136. *See also* Intersect,
        Union
    transforming events 142–143. *See also*
        Transform events
Route feature class
    creating
        in a geodatabase 54
        in an existing feature dataset 57
    defined 157

Route identifier
    creating an index 57, 59
    defined 157
    described 78
    saving 78
    setting 21, 35, 78, 82
    values 80
Route location
    defined 157
    described 44, 107
    finding 24, 82
    identifying 23, 80
    labeling 81
Route measure. *See also* Route measures
    defined 157
Route measure anomalies
    defined 157
    described 25, 104
    displaying 25, 104
        using a scale range 104
        using a SQL query 104
Route measure units
    converting 36
Route measures. *See also* Measures
    calculating using points 50. *See also*
        Calibrating routes
    editing
        with an edit sketch 121
    setting 119
        using Apply Factor 120
        using Calculate NaN 120
        using Drop Measures 120
        using Offset 120
        using Set As Distance 119
        using Set Direction as M 120
        using Set From/To 120
Route reference. *See also* Linear referencing
        method
    defined 157
    multiple 129
    using one not in the map 144

Route structure 142
Routes
  calibrating with points 67–69
  creating 111
    by merging linear features 48
    from existing lines 61–62
  defined 157
  described 43, 48
  editing 32
  making from selected features 34, 111
  realigning 122
  recalibrating 37
  remeasuring 123
  storing 48

S

Scale
  defined 157
Segmented data 41
Selected set
  defined 158
Shapefile
  creating to store routes 58
  defined 158
Shortest path distance 67. *See* Calibrating
    routes
Shotpoint
  described 5
Simple route
  creating 111
Sketch
  defined 158
Snapping environment
  defined 158
Spatial bookmark
  defined 158
Spatial domain
  defined 158
Spatial reference
  defined 158

SQL
  defined 158
Standalone feature class
  creating to store routes 54–57
Starting priority. *See* Coordinate priority
Stationing
  defined 158
Storing routes 48
Symbol
  defined 158

T

Table
  defined 158
  noneditable 150
Target annotation
  nonappearing 98
Target feature class
  setting 33
Tolerance
  choosing 142
Toolbars
  adding 33
Topology 45
  defined 158
  described 45
  with multiple linear referencing methods 45
Transform events. *See also* Route events
  defined 158

U

Union
  defined 159
  events. *See* Overlay events
Universal Transverse Mercator (UTM)
  defined 159
UTM (Universal Transverse Mercator)
  defined 159
  described 43

V

Vector
  defined 159
  described 40
Vector model
  defined 159
  described 41
Vertex
  defined 159

W

Wizard
  defined 159
Workspace
  creating 135
  defined 159

Z

Zero length line event
  defined 159
  described 147